I0114660

RISING TIDE, RESILIENT VOICES:

BANGLADESHI WOMEN BATTLING
CLIMATE CHANGE

MUMITA TANJEELA, PHD

CG COMMON GROUND

First published in 2025
as part of the **Climate Change: Impacts and Responses Book Imprint**
Common Ground Research Networks

University of Illinois Research Park
2001 South First St, Suite 201 L
Champaign, IL 61820 USA

Copyright © Mumita Tanjeela, 2025

All rights reserved. Apart from fair dealing for the purposes of study, research, criticism or review as permitted under the applicable copyright legislation, no part of this book may be reproduced by any process without writ-ten permission from the publisher.

Library of Congress Cataloging-in-Publication Data

Names:Tanjeela, Mumita author Title: Rising tide, resilient voices : Bangladeshi women battling climate change / Mumita Tanjeela. Description: Champaign, IL : Common Ground Research Networks, 2025. Summary: "Climate change is a pressing global concern, with Bangladesh ranking as the sixth most vulnerable country due to its geography. The nation faces extreme weather events, including sea-level rise, saltwater intrusion, storms, floods, and droughts, with poverty exacerbating these issues. Women bear a disproportionate burden, as environmental degradation affects their family's survival directly. While men often migrate for livelihoods, women develop resilience strategies that can inform successful climate adaptation programs. This book delves into the gender aspect of climate change response in Bangladesh, examining adaptation strategies from various stakeholders. It emphasizes the need to recognize women not just as victims but as active agents in climate adaptation. Despite vulnerability assessments, limited research explores the unique contributions women can make in this context. The book presents women's narratives and the impact of intra-household power dynamics on their mobility and resource access. The research highlights the gap between policy and practice, emphasizing the importance of gender mainstreaming in climate adaptation efforts in Bangladesh. This work encourages further exploration of gender dimensions in climate change adaptation, both theoretically and empirically"-- Provided by publisher.

Identifiers: LCCN 2025004921 (print) | LCCN 2025004922 (ebook) | ISBN 9781966214274 hardback | ISBN 9781966214281 paperback | ISBN 9781966214298 adobe pdf

Subjects: LCSH: Women and the environment--Bangladesh | Climatic changes--Social aspects--Bangladesh | Climate change adaptation--Bangladesh | Bangladesh--Environmental conditions Classification: LCC GF696.B3 T36 2025 (print) | LCC GF696.B3 (ebook) | DDC 363.7/0525082095492--dc23/eng/20250508 LC record available at https://lccn.loc.gov/2025004921 LC ebook record available at https://lccn.loc.gov/2025004922

TABLE OF CONTENTS

Preface   *vii*

Acknowledgments   *ix*

Summary   *xi*

Chapter 1: Climate Change Impacts and Vulnerable
Sectors in Bangladesh   1

Chapter 2: Theoretical Framework and Methodology of the Study   15

Chapter 3: Gender Relations and Climate Change: Suffering
of Women in Bangladesh   41

Chapter 4: Women's Responses to Climate Change
at the Household Level   51

Chapter 5: Women's Responses to Community-Based Adaptation   61

Chapter 6: Stories of Climate Champions   69

Chapter 7: Climate Change Adaptation in Bangladesh—Policy
Frameworks Through Gender Lens   87

Chapter 8: Conclusions: Resilience and Adaptation—Fostering
Gender Equality   103

Bibliography   *111*

List of Maps

1. Locations of the Programs Chosen for the Study in Bangladesh   22
2. Cyclone Affected Areas of BD   24
3. Location of Khulna and Bagerhat Districts   25
4. Drought Map of Bangladesh   28
5. Location of Naogaon District   29
6. Location of Cox's Bazar District   32
7. Flood Water Map of Bangladesh   34
8. Location Map of Gopalganj District   35

List of Tables

1. Representative Year for 10 and 20 Years Return Period   4
2. Top 10 Most Vulnerable Drought Spots in Bangladesh   5
3. High Risk Areas Inundated by Tidal Surge (Height 1 m)   7
4. Different Types of Disaster and Livelihood Vulnerabilities   13
5. Research Methods Used to Collect Data and Information   38
6. Gender Segregation of the Interviewees   39
7. Selected Indicators of Gender Relation in Bangladesh   52

Glossary

Gono Gobeshona Dol	village research group
Haor	a wetland ecosystem in the northeastern part of Bangladesh
Khas Land	government-owned land
Mohila Somiti	women's group
Mutha Sonchoy	handful rice saving
Nari Bikash Kendra	women development forum
Union	unit of upazila
Upazila	sub-district

PREFACE

My doctoral research thesis, completed in 2016, has been preserved with the anticipation of potential publications in journals and book chapters. Since its initial completion, several publications, including articles and book chapters, have already emanated from the wealth of research contained within the thesis. The dormant state of this work underwent a transformative shift when Common Ground Research Networks expressed keen interest in adapting it into a comprehensive book.

During the preparation of the book manuscript, certain necessary updates were made to the available secondary data to enhance its relevance. I extend my heartfelt appreciation to Common Ground Research Networks. Their unwavering support and interest in transforming this research into a book have been instrumental in broadening the reach of this study to a wider audience. Their commitment to making this publication a reality has been invaluable, and I express my sincere thanks for the opportunity they have provided to share this research on a larger scale.

ACKNOWLEDGMENTS

I would like to express my sincere gratitude to my advisors, Dr. Giorel Curran and Dr. Elizabeth van Acker, for their invaluable guidance, advice, and unwavering attention during the progression of my thesis. Their profound interest in the topic, exceptional supervisory skills, and academic insights were instrumental. Despite their heavy workload, their positive encouragement, patience in reviewing chapters, and pleasant personalities provided me with moral strength and kept me motivated throughout this study. I owe them a great deal for their crucial support, without which completing my thesis on time would not have been possible. Special thanks to Professor Andrew O'Neil, head of the School of Government and International Relations, and Professor Haig Patapan, director of the Centre of Governance and Public Policy, for supporting me with the completion scholarship and financial assistance for overseas fieldwork. Gratitude also extends to our office staff members, Julie Howe and Angela MacDonald, whose exceptional support eased my journey. I am truly thankful to Griffith University for making my dream a reality through the International Postgraduate Research Scholarship (IPRS). I am deeply appreciative of Dr. Shannon Rutherford, Associate Professor in the School of Medicine, Griffith University, Australia, for her immense interest in climate change and gender issues in Bangladesh. Her constructive inputs, suggestions, and comments were pivotal in shaping my research. Special acknowledgment is due to Daniela di Piramo for her meticulous editing of my thesis.

My thanks to PhD colleagues, especially Lucy West and Caitlin Mollica, for their continuous support in reviewing my writing despite their busy schedules. I am indebted to my friend Anisur Rahman for guiding me in selecting fields and projects for my study. I extend my gratitude to office colleagues Afifa and Shahin for their mental support in dealing with official matters. Special thanks to field colleagues who provided assistance during my fieldwork in Bangladesh. I am grateful to the Ministry of Women and Children Affairs (MoWCA) and the Department of Women Affairs (DWA) for granting me a 4-year deputation for my PhD studies. A heartfelt thank-you to the staff members of selected NGOs and all participants in interviews and FGDs (who remain anonymous) for their cooperation and valuable time. I acknowledge the care and support of friends in Australia and Bangladesh during my stay away from home.

I share my joy with my nieces, Raya and Fiona, and express gratitude to my brother Sourov, sisters Mousumi and Rimi, and brothers-in-law for their continuous encouragement in my higher studies. Finally, I dedicate my book to my exceptional parents, expressing deep respect and gratitude for their affection, moral support, and confidence in my decisions. Their wishes have always been my key strength throughout this journey.

SUMMARY

Climate change has become a globally critical concern. The 21st century will pose significant challenges due to the escalating impacts of climate change (Intergovernmental Panel on Climate Change [IPCC], 2023). Bangladesh, as a developing country in South Asia, is ranked the seventh most vulnerable nation globally due to its geographical settings (GCRI, 2021). The country is confronted with extreme climatic events, including sea level rise, saltwater intrusion into arable lands, and an increased risk of severe storms, cyclones, floods, flash floods, and drought in the coming years. The nexus between poverty and climate change is a major concern, particularly in Bangladesh, where a lack of resources poses a significant problem in both rural and urban areas. Consequently, climate vulnerability in Bangladesh is closely tied to poverty, shaping its adaptation capacity.

Various communities in Bangladesh, such as those living in coastal zones, drought-prone areas, settlers on unstable slopes, and climate refugees in urban slums, are affected by climate change. Among these affected groups, women emerge as more vulnerable than men to the impacts of climate change, evident from the country's history of climate-induced disasters. Climate change amplifies women's socio-economic vulnerabilities by directly affecting their families' food security, water consumption, and traditional livelihoods. Environmental degradation, according to Jahan (2008), disproportionately affects women as the survival of their families, for which they are responsible, depends directly on the natural resource base. While men often migrate in search of new livelihoods, women are left behind to support their families, prompting them to develop coping and resilience strategies to survive the impacts of climate change.

Against this backdrop, this book explores the gender dimension of the climate change response in Bangladesh by examining various adaptation strategies initiated by communities, government agencies, and development stakeholders. My study revealed how gender has been incorporated or neglected in these adaptation programs and argues that women, rather than being portrayed solely as victims of climate change, possess skills and knowledge crucial for successful and sustainable climate change adaptation efforts. Previous studies on climate change adaptation in Bangladesh have often overlooked the gender dimension. While identifying vulnerable groups, including women, the research has generally not delved into the specific contributions women could make in climate change adaptation, particularly in Bangladesh.

This is a country case study, employing the fundamental ideas of feminist political ecology, ecofeminism, and feminist environmentalism. It adopted a qualitative approach, utilizing a case study and multi-methods approach to explore climate change impacts in four regions of Bangladesh—covering both rural and urban contexts: salinity and cyclones in the Khulna region, drought in the Naogaon district, landslides in Cox's Bazar municipality, and flooding in the Gopalganj district.

The book presents women's narratives, providing deeper insights into how women build resilience at the household level and how this resilience extends to a macro level. It emphasized the substantial influence of "intra-household power dynamics" on women's mobility, endowments, and access to and control over resources. Considering these power dynamics is critical when involving women in formal adaptation programs, and hence the gap between policy implementation and practice, underscoring the need for gender mainstreaming in climate change adaptation processes in Bangladesh highlighted in the book.

CHAPTER 1

Climate Change Impacts and Vulnerable Sectors in Bangladesh

Introduction

Climate change can be defined as the geo-hydro-meteorological change to climate that manifests itself through multi-dimensional and multi-longitudinal socio-environmental consequences (O'Brien et al., 2006, p. 68). The *Sixth Synthesis Report of the Intergovernmental Panel on Climate Change* (IPCC, 2023) claims that global climate has already been warming at an unprecedented rate in the past 200 years. It states that "widespread and rapid changes in the atmosphere, ocean, cryosphere and biosphere have occurred. Human-caused climate change is already affecting many weather and climate extremes in every region across the globe. This has led to widespread adverse impacts and related losses and damages to nature and people (high confidence)" (IPCC, 2023, p. 5). The changing trend is apparent through extreme weather events, average sea-level rise, snow cover and ice decline, frequent natural hazards, and environmental degradation. However, the potential impact of climate change is intensifying social and economic problems in natural resource-dependent developing countries that are more vulnerable to climate change (Adger et al., 2003). Climate change has led to widespread and unevenly distributed adverse impacts, causing economic damages in climate-exposed sectors like agriculture, forestry, fishery, energy, and tourism. Individuals have experienced disruptions in livelihoods through destruction of homes and infrastructure, loss of property and income, and adverse effects on human health, food security, as well as gender and social equity (IPCC, 2023). It is also the case that even if both developed and developing countries are being affected, developing and underdeveloped countries are the most vulnerable to the threat of climate change due to its direct impact on their agriculture, natural resources, as well as their overall poor economic and social development sectors (Adaptation Knowledge Platform [AKP],[1] 2010; International Institute for Strategic Studies [IISS], 2000).

Climate Change and Bangladesh

The potential, and existing, impacts of climate change position Bangladesh as one of the major climate changes affected countries in the world. The Global Climate Risk Index (GCRI, 2021) indicates that Bangladesh is the seventh most vulnerable country in the world, facing extreme climatic events resulting from climate change; this includes 1.20 percent of GDP losses and 228 disasters events during the last 20 years (1994–2013) alone. Due to its geographical setting Bangladesh is facing climatic hazards such as sea level rise, saltwater intrusions in arable lands and increased natural disasters such as powerful cyclones, storms surges, seasonal floods, flash floods, and prolonged droughts (Bangladesh Climate Change Strategy and Action Plan [BCCSAP], 2009, p. 4; Hijioka et al., 2014, pp. 1347–1350). It is projected that a 45-cm sea-level rise would lead to a potential loss of 10 percent of land, which would affect 15 percent of the country's population (United Nations Development Programme [UNDP], 2007, p. 12) and is likely to increase poverty by 15 percent by 2030 (Hijioka et al., 2014, p. 1349). In addition, most of the visible adverse effects of climate change are likely to lead to large-scale damage to crops and water resources, loss of livelihood, employment and an overall negative impact on the national economy of Bangladesh (Delaporte and Maurel, 2016; Choudhury et al., 2005; Climate Change Cell [CCC], 2009b). The fast-growing urban slums where the urban poor mostly live is another vulnerable sector of Bangladesh (Tanjeela and Billah, 2022; BCCSAP, 2009). The nexus between poverty and climate change is a major concern, especially in a country like Bangladesh where lack of resources is a foremost issue in both rural and urban areas. The following sections discuss the visible scenarios of climate change in Bangladesh, focusing on changing weather patterns, climate variability and common climatic hazards or disasters.

---

[1] The Regional Climate Change Adaptation Knowledge Platform for Asia referred to as the "Adaptation Knowledge Platform" has been developed to respond to the demand for effective mechanisms for sharing information on climate change adaptation and developing adaptive capacities in Asian countries, many of which are the most vulnerable to the effects of climate change. The study report (AKP, 2010) was prepared by this platform.

Visible Impacts of Climate Change in Bangladesh

Flooding

Across the world, Bangladesh is considered the sixth most flood-prone country (UNDP as cited in Azad et al., 2013, p. 190), and during the last 25 years, six major floods have damaged its socio-economic system and infrastructure severely (BCCSAP, 2009, p. 9). Due to the convergence of the Ganges, Brahmaputra, and Meghna (GBM) river basins, an average annual flood inundates 20.5 percent of the country, whereas during an extreme flood event, such as that in 1988 and 1998, it can reach about 70 percent (Mirza, 2002, p. 128; World Bank [WB], 2010, p. xii). About two-thirds of the country is lower than 5 m above the sea level, with an average river slope of 6 cm/km in the delta; consequently it is at risk of river and tidal flooding (BCCSAP, 2009, p. 7; WB, 2010, p. xi). However, floods in Bangladesh are classified into four categories based on their origin: river floods, rainwater floods, coastal floods, and flash floods (Mirza, 2002, p. 128). The World Bank (2010, p. 11) states that "nearly 80 percentage of the country's annual precipitation occurs during the summer monsoon, when these rivers have a combined peak flow of 180,000 m³/sec, the second highest in the world." Consequently, about 80 percent of the country's total areas are at risk of various types of flood (Mirza et al., 2003, p. 304). In addition, low lying coastal areas are exposed to 15.3 percent more tidal or surge flood risk as recent impacts of climate change (Karim and Mimura, 2008, p. 490). Choudhury et al. (2005, p. 16) argue that increased monsoon precipitations, higher water flows in rivers, and sea-level rise combinedly increase the depth and extent of flood inundation. According to the Bangladesh Disaster Report (2011):

> Once upon a time a natural flood was called the "blessing of God" because the soil benefits from flood. The alluvium which comes with flood water increases the fertility of the land. But unusual flood and waterlogging is changing all the calculations. (2011, p. 9)

The Comprehensive Disaster Management Programme (CDMP, 2014c) identifies 17 districts in Bangladesh that have a history of 10-to-20-year return period of annual floods; more areas are likely to be exposed to higher inundation in the changing climate with increased precipitation and sea-level rise. The flood map produced by the CDMP (2014c) shows three different water level stations from three basins for a 10- and 20-year return period of floods in Table 1.

Table 1: Representative Year for 10- and 20-Year Return Period

River Basin	Representative Year for 10-Year Return Period	Representative Year for 20-Year Return Period
Brahmaputra	1995	2007
Ganges	1987	1998
Meghna	1988	1998

Source: Impact Assessment of Climate Change and Sea Level Rise on Monsoon Flooding, CDMP (2014c, p. 17).

Mirza (2002, p. 127) argues that due to global warming there will be an extensive impact on the hydrology and water resources of the river basins where Bangladesh is situated that ultimately will lead to more flooding. However, as a consequence of climate change Bangladesh is already exposed to all types of flooding, something that will continue to place its population, economy and infrastructure at increasing risk (Mirza et al., 2003, p. 315).

Drought

Drought is another climate related problem in the north and north-west part of Bangladesh as a consequence of anthropogenic intervention (Shahid, 2008, p. 2235). Drought is defined as a prolonged and continuous period of dry weather along with erratic and insufficient rainfall (Ahmed et al., 1999). In the last 50 years, Bangladesh has experienced 19 severe drought events (Habiba et al., 2012, p. 73; Selvaraju et al., 2006, p. 1). Although it is a regular phenomenon in some parts of the country, the north-west region is facing more drought events (CDMP, 2013). It is evident that this region is receiving much lower annual rainfall compared to the rest of the country, which is 2,044 mm mostly in the monsoon period. Moreover, this area experiences a huge temperature difference between the summer (45°C) and winter (5°C) seasons (Habiba et al., 2013; Paul, 1995, 1998; Shahid, 2008, p. 2236). Depending on the current precipitation trend and rainfall variability, Shahid (2008, p. 2245) predicts an increased severity of droughts in the near future in this part of Bangladesh. However, along with rainfall trends, other reasons identified for drought include a lower amount of discharge from major rivers, drying water channels and declining groundwater levels (Shahid and Behrawan, 2008, p. 393).

Initially, Karim et al. (1990) prepared a drought risk map where "cumulative effect of dry days, higher temperatures during pre-monsoon periods and low soil moisture availability" were identified as reasons. Afterward, Water Resource Planning Organization (WAPRO) prepared another map identifying drought-prone zones during winter and the pre-monsoon period in 1996 (cited in Shahid and Behrawan, 2008, p. 392). In 2000, the Bangladesh Agricultural Research Council (BARC) produced a more detailed seasonal drought map based on the rabi (monsoon), kharif II (pre-monsoon) and kharif ll (post-monsoon) periods in Bangladesh and identified the most vulnerable drought-prone areas or hot spots (see Table 2) from the combined vulnerability ranking (Ahmed, 2006, p. 21; CDMP, 2013, p. 25). All of the maps identified the north and north-west regions of Bangladesh as more prone to drought.

Table 2: Top 10 Most Vulnerable Drought Spots in Bangladesh

District	Upazila	Vulnerability Ranking			Combined Rank	Severity Ranking
		Rabi	Kharif I	Kharif II		
Naogaon	Niamatpur	7	5	3	15	1
Rajshahi	Tanore	6	5	11	19	2
Nawabganj	Nachole	9	5	4	20	3
Naogaon	Porsha	4	5	16	23	4
Naogaon	Sapahar	5	2	17	26	5
Thakurgaon	Baliadangi			30	30	6
Dinajpur	Hakimpur	18		12	30	7
Naogaon	Patnitala	12	18	1	31	8
Nawabganj	Shibganj	11	5	14	33	9
Joypurhat	Panchbibi	36		2	38	10

Source: Vulnerability to Climate-Induced Drought Scenario and Impact (CDMP, 2013, p. 25).

Shahid and Behrawan (2008, p. 392) argue that Bangladesh is a unique case with a combination of drought and flood. However, although drought impact is more severe than flood in many cases, it is yet to be considered as a major hazard.

Cyclones and Tidal Surges

Bangladesh, particularly its long coastline, is severely exposed to tropical cyclones along with tidal surges (Islam and Peterson, 2009, p. 115). Bangladesh experiences severe cyclone strikes every three years on average accompanied by high wind and storm surges (BCCSAP, 2009, p. 11). According to the IPCC (2007), due to climate change Bangladesh is expected to face increased severity of cyclones by 2050 along with sea-level rise and storm surges. Karim and Mimura (2008, p. 490) state that "the country is likely to be affected by more intense cyclonic events in the foreseeable future due to climate change and sea-level rise (SLR)." While storm surges are usually less than 10 m, Bangladesh often experiences surges of above 10 m (WB, 2010, p. xi). Between 1877 and 2003, Bangladesh was hit by 117 cyclones, including 52 severe cyclonic storms and 39 tropical depressions; of these, 26 were of hurricane category (Islam and Peterson, 2009, p. 118). Another report shows that 19 strong cyclones hit the coastal belt of Bangladesh from 1960 to 2012 (CDMP, 2014c, p. 11). Sidr, a category 4 cyclone, hit southern Bangladesh in November 2007 and killed 3,500 people, displaced another 2 million and caused huge crop and economic loss and cyclone Aila caused huge crop damage while 1,500 people lost their lives (Dastagir, 2015, p. 49). A study by the CDMP (2014c, p. 11) shows that a coastal area of 19,146 sq. km in Bangladesh is already inundated by water depth of more than 1 m at the base as a result of the tidal surges of cyclones. According to that study (CDMP, 2014c, pp. 13–15) the highly impacted hazard area is defined as the area that experiences inundation depth of 1 m or more, human casualties, and damage to crops and infrastructure. Table 3 presents the areas of inundation in comparison with the base conditions.

The life experiences of local people and relevant studies suggest that the characteristics of tropical cyclones in terms of intensity and frequency have changed over the years in Bangladesh. Moreover, the geographic and demographic conditions of the country will lead to more devastation from these types of disastrous events.

Table 3: High Risk Areas Inundated by Tidal Surge (Height 1 m)

	Regions (Area in Square Kilometers)		
Scenarios	South-West	South-East	Eastern Hill
Base condition	14,038.24	2,916.92	2,191.72
Climate change condition	15,055.32	3,299.76	2,390.88
Additional risk area due to climate change	1,017.08	382.84	199.16

Source: Policy Brief–Local Level Hazards Map for Flood, Storm and Salinity, CDMP (2014c, p. 11).

Landslides

Landslides have been a recent addition to the list of natural hazards in Bangladesh. Although Bangladesh is basically a country with a flat topography, the south-east part is hilly and mountainous with a number of terraces which cover 18 percent of it (Mahmood and Khan, 2008). A number of these hilly districts have experienced severe landslide incidents in recent years (Displacement Solutions, 2012, p. 12). Bangladesh is the fifth most vulnerable country for landslide-induced fatalities in Asia (Kjekstad and Highland, 2009, p. 574). A study by the CDMP (2012b, p. 2) explains that landslides are caused by the exposure of soft sedimentary rocks due to interventions by human activities across the slopes in conjunction with torrential monsoon rainfall. In addition, heavy downpours over a short spell led to landslides in both natural and man-made slopes in the rainy season (CCC, 2007, p. 1). Kjekstad and Highland confirm that most of the landslides occur due to climatic factors such as change of rainfall patterns and human intervention and often cause migration and unplanned new settlements (2009, p. 574). A total number of 147 landslides occurred during 1995–2010 with hundreds of human fatalities in Cox's Bazar alone (CDMP, 2012a, pp. 10–12). It is evident that the hazards range from small-scale to large-scale depending on the flow of rain and the vulnerability of the slopes, but ultimately, they all cause significant damage to live and properties. Frequent landslides are likely to result in huge population displacement from the hilly regions of Bangladesh in the near future (Displacement Solutions, 2012, p. 12). A hazard like landslides is one of the outcomes of land use patterns and unplanned urban settlement from those displaced by climate change and who subsequently seek refuge in nearby urban areas

Vulnerable Sectors

According to a study by the WB (2010, p. 12), the severity of the 1998 flood caused over US$2 billion economic loss including loss of agriculture, infrastructure, industry and people's livelihood, equating to 4.8 percent of the country's GDP. Furthermore, in 2007, Cyclone Sidr triggered huge damage and losses in the coastal region of Bangladesh, accounting for US$1.7 billion economic loss and reducing the GDP by 2.6 percent (WB, 2012). These two hazards are but "small" instances of the severity of climate change impacts on the economy of Bangladesh. The next section summarizes the potential effects of climate change on different socio-economic sectors of Bangladesh. The sectors are discussed according to the significance of vulnerabilities and their interconnectivities.

Agriculture and Food Security

In Bangladesh, 64.1 percent of people living in rural areas are directly or indirectly engaged in a wide range of agricultural activities (Alam, 2015, p. 196). Agriculture is a key economic sector in Bangladesh: it accounts for 23.5 percent of the country's GDP and engages more than 62 percent of the country's labor force; 80 percent of rural people survive on agricultural activities (Habiba et al., 2013, p. 72). Crop production is the prime activity of agriculture and in it rice is the main crop, accounting for about 80 percent of total crops and being cultivated 3 times/year (Ruane et al., 2013, p. 340). The agricultural sector is heavily dependent on climate, which means that changes in temperatures and the amount of rainfall affect its production directly. According to the WB (2010, p. xvii) "the combined effects of rising temperatures, higher precipitation, CO_2 fertilization, severe flooding, occasional seasonal droughts, and loss of arable land in coastal areas resulting from climate change are expected to result in declines in rice production of 3.9 percent each year, or a cumulative total of 80 million tons over 2005–50." Similarly, Ruane et al. (2013, p. 342) argue that agricultural sectors in Bangladesh experience reduced crop production as a consequence of changes in temperature, precipitation, CO_2 concentrations, and solar radiation.

According to Karim (1995, p. 253), a severe drought in 1989 in the north Bengal region affected the livelihoods and food security of 50,000 people, particularly through a huge loss of agricultural production. In addition, recurring severe droughts have substantial impacts on rice production, which can be reduced by 45–60 percent, while for other crops the reduction can range from 50 to 70 percent (Habiba et al., 2012, p. 73). On the other hand, Habibullah et al., (1999, p. 63) assert that salinity intrusion in arable land can reduce a crop by 0.2 t/ha of land.

The impact of climate change on the agricultural sector is considered the most serious compared to other sectors because it affects the livelihood and food security of a significant proportion of the population (Gebrehiwot and Veen, 2013). Alam (2015, p. 199) claims that "droughts and water scarcity are expected to be more frequent, particularly in southwest Bangladesh…which will ultimately affect the agricultural economy and rural livelihoods and threaten hard-earned food security." It is evident that recurring crop loss leads to loss of income and livelihood-related problems such as food insecurity, seasonal food crises (famine), malnutrition, deteriorating health conditions (both physical and mental) and increased domestic violence (Ekpoh, 1999; Habiba et al., 2012; Nasreen, 2008a). Nasreen et al. (2013) argue that the landless agricultural laborer is marginalized and that subsistence farmers in rural Bangladesh are the most insecure group because they suffer more from different climatic events, something which ultimately leads to loss of income and increased poverty.

Impact on Water Resources

Climate change's impact on water resources is another critical consideration for Bangladesh, as water is an essential element for life and livelihood, and insecurity of supply is particularly felt in coastal belts, riverine flood-prone areas, and drought-prone areas. Both population pressures and the impact of climate change expose the vulnerabilities of water resources. Alam (2015) argues that delayed monsoons and uneven distribution of rainfall leads to water unavailability and increased water scarcity. As a consequence, the use of groundwater, especially for irrigation purposes, has increased in Bangladesh since 1980, particularly during the cultivation period which has contributed to a significant decrease in surface and groundwater (Shamsuddoha et al., 2012, p. 910).

Increased flooding is another cause of the extreme water problems that Bangladesh has been experiencing in both coastal and inland areas over the years.

In addition, water availability depends highly on monsoonal rainfall and seasonal variability; consequently, both humans and ecosystems suffer considerably in the dry season (Ahmed, 2006; UNDP, 2007). Bangladesh's annual precipitation has been significantly reduced in the dry season, which has made the south-west and north-west regions of the country drought prone. The drought situation leads to scarcity of water for both irrigation and household consumption and creates associated vulnerabilities (Agrawala et al., 2003).

Bangladesh Climate Change Country Study (1997) demonstrates that scarcity of water resources has increased due to a combination of sea-level rise and water flow during rainy seasons. It also found that the lower Ganges and the Surma floodplains are more vulnerable compared to other areas in the era of climate change in Bangladesh (see also Alam et al., 1998). Salinity intrusion, especially contamination of drinking water sources in coastal belts, appears to be the most important concern for the locality, especially for women (CCC, 2009a). According to Rahman and Mahbub (2012), water management has become a more complicated issue for the southern part of Bangladesh, as saline water has inundated the surface as well as the groundwater systems. This impacts adversely on traditional agricultural production and also on human health. The BCCSAP (2009) acknowledges that:

> Shortage of safe drinking water is likely to become more pronounced, especially in the coastal belt and in drought-prone areas in the north-west of the country. This will impose hardship on women and children, who are responsible for collecting drinking water for their families. Increasingly saline drinking water may also result in health hazards, especially for pregnant women. Climate change is likely to adversely affect women more than men. (2009, p. 13)

These water resource problems are creating multifaceted impacts on the lives and livelihood of affected populations.

Lives and Livelihood

With Bangladesh being one of the most densely populated countries, it is anticipated that climate change will exacerbate the country's overall socio-economic vulnerabilities at a critical level. The increasing trends of weather change and natural hazards in recent decades have made affected communities vulnerable in diverse ways (Atiq et al., 2007; CCC, 2009a). In particular, poor people dependent on nature are at risk of losing assets, livelihood, and employment that are essential for their survival and coping capacity (Tariqul et al., 2015, p. 4). According to Nasreen et al. (2013, p. 11), people from the coastal regions of Bangladesh are continuously fighting against the adverse impacts of climate change and they have to survive without any employment for more than 4 months/year on average. Dastagir (2015) demonstrates that different climate change impacts not only reduce livelihood options but also have the potential to destroy assets such as houses, livestock, plantations, and local resource bases. The National Adaptation Plan of Action (NAPA, 2005, p. 16) describes livelihood vulnerability in terms of negative impact on employment, income, and consumption (including food security) for various groups in society. The degree of exposure depends upon their initial economic conditions (poor or non-poor), location (coastal or non-coastal, rural, or urban), and gender. A study by Pouliotte et al. (2009, p. 38) demonstrates the environmental vulnerability due to the direct impact of salinity intrusion on poor people's lives in terms of freshwater availability and loss of traditional agriculture and natural resources. These losses reduce their livelihood options and push them below the poverty line. Similar situations were revealed during my field visits when local people confirmed that they lost their traditional livelihood, particularly agriculture, and have few survival alternatives.

Poor health is another important impact of climate change on Bangladeshi people's lives. The unavailability of safe water, food insecurity, and environmental degradation directly impact the health of the poor people in both rural and urban areas (BCCSAP, 2009, p. 16). Many types of health-related problems such as diarrhea, cholera, typhoid, high blood pressure, anxiety, and malnutrition are common consequences of climate change in Bangladesh (Alston, 2015). These types of health risks vary depending on the socio-economic conditions of the population, but disadvantaged groups are more vulnerable than others. The adverse impacts of climate change fall disproportionately on the most vulnerable groups within the country as a whole.

Climate-Induced Displacement/Migration

There is a high probability that a large number of climate refugees will emerge in Bangladesh, due to some of the climate change impacts that we have discussed thus far. Sea-level rise is one of these, which poses a great threat for the coastal population. The BCCSAP (2009, p. 14) suspects that if sea levels rise more than the current trend then "six to eight million people could be displaced by 2050 and would have to be resettled." The United Nations predicts that a three-feet sea-level rise in the next 50 years would lead to the disappearance of a quarter of Bangladesh's coastline and 30 million Bangladeshis would be displaced from their homes and land (as cited in Dastagir, 2015, p. 49). Similar projections have been made by Choudhury et al. (2005) and the BCCSAP (2009) who note that the scale and frequency of extreme climate events have been steadily increasing, making people's lives difficult and leading to increasing displacement from their homes and lands. Latest household income and expenditure survey (HIES, 2022) reveals that the migration rate is higher in rural areas compared to urban areas, standing at 11.64 and 7.98 percent, respectively.

A study by the Association for Climate Refugees (ACR, 2012, p. 547) claims that in Bangladesh a total of 6.5 million people have already been displaced and almost half of them have been displaced by tidal floods and riverbank erosion. According to the Displacement Solution (2012, p. 5), in 236 coastal upazilas tidal floods and sea-level rise have forced 64 percent of inhabitants to move to local embankments or higher grounds, while 27 percent of the population has been displaced to other areas within the country. In addition, due to riverbank erosion, 42 percent of the population has been locally displaced, whereas 26 percent of inhabitants have moved to urban slums including Dhaka city from 179 upazilas (mainland areas) of Bangladesh. A recent report by Hasan (2015) claims that approximately 350,000 people migrate to Dhaka city from all over the country annually, driven by climate change incidents and a hope for better employment opportunities. As a result, the urban population of Bangladesh is increasing rapidly and currently stands at 35 percent of the total population (WB, 2015). This trend is making these urban centers unstable, particularly Dhaka and Chittagong where climate refugees are moving to access greater economic and employment opportunities. The BCCSAP (2009, p. 16) warns that Bangladesh is going to face an "urgent and pressing problem" due to rapid and unplanned urbanization.

In Bangladesh, two types of population migration are common. The first one is migration driven by poverty that includes temporary, short- or long-term, and seasonal migration due to economic reasons (Afsar, 2003; Qin, 2010; Khandker, 2012); and the second is human mobility due to environmental degradation (Ahsan et al., 2011; Gray and Mueller, 2012; Mallick and Vogt, 2014). However,

Mallick and Vogt (2014, p. 209) argue that both social and environmental drivers combine to influence affected populations to disperse from vulnerable places. In order to show the link between population mobility and natural disasters, Gray and Mueller (2012, p. 6004) note that households that live in severely climate-affected areas are most likely to migrate to other locations. However, the most vulnerable households not only experience significant barriers to moving but also lack substantial local adaptive capacity. The poor and marginalized groups, particularly small or subsistence farmers, agricultural laborers, fishing communities, and some natural resource-dependent communities, face more difficulties from climate change in Bangladesh (Easterling et al., 2007). In addition, they are confronted with a "double dilemma," since their lives are more reliant on agriculture and local ecology, which are directly affected by climate change, and they have fewer options and capacity to take the necessary measures to adapt (Shamsuddoha et al., 2012, p. 24).

Table 4 provides a depiction of different types of disasters and the impacts on the livelihood of people. The table was developed from information gathered from secondary literature as well as my empirical findings.

Climate change has clearly manifested itself through a range of weather events and climatic hazards in Bangladesh. As an Asian developing country and one

Table 4: Different Types of Disaster and Livelihood Vulnerabilities

Type of Hazards	*Livelihood Vulnerability*
Flood	Reduces livelihood options due to loss of agriculture, health hazards, water logging, scarcity of fresh water
Drought	Loss of agricultural activities, unemployment, illness due to extreme heat, water scarcity, migration for new livelihood
Cyclone and storm surges	Limits fishing time in the Bay, loss of life and assets
Sea-level rise	Salinity intrusion, crop loss, loss of traditional livelihood options, lack of fresh water, forced displacement
Landslides	Lack of safety and security, lack of quality of life, less income opportunity

of the most adversely affected by climate change, Bangladesh is facing diverse climate change effects such as sea-level rises, increased tropical cyclones, salinity intrusion in arable lands, intensified droughts, precipitation variability and frequent flooding. In Bangladesh climate is not merely an environmental phenomenon but is also interconnected with many socio-cultural and economic factors. These create increased vulnerabilities for a major group of the population. Evidence from a global perspective has revealed that natural resources-based and agriculture-dependent populations are the primary victims of climate change. More than one-third of the population of Bangladesh lives in rural areas and they are the main drivers of the rural agriculture-based economy of the country (Bangladesh Bureau of Statistics [BBS], 2011). Therefore, climate events directly and indirectly endanger these people's lives in multifaceted ways and make their lives extremely arduous.

CHAPTER 2

Theoretical Framework and Methodology of the Study

For the last two decades, both ecofeminists and feminist environmentalist scholars have been arguing that during any environmental degradation, women are the most adversely affected due to their biological and social roles as care givers (Mallory, 2010; Gaard and Gruen, 2005; Buckingham-Hatfield, 2000; Mellor, 1997; Jackson, 1993; Dobscha, 1993). One distinction is that while the ecofeminists emphasize the spiritual connection between women and nature, the proponents of feminist environmentalism argue instead that women's connection with nature is more concrete or materialist and takes place throughout their life due to their closer proximity to the natural environment (Agarwal, 2009). Feminist political ecology, on the other hand, is a subfield of political ecology which examines the gendered dimension of environmental crises from a broader institutional perspective involving government, politics, and other institutions that shape the overall social system (Rocheleau et al., 1996; Hovorka, 2006). It offers an analytical framework to establish the argument that ecological concerns cannot be understood unless linked to political economy (Sundberg, 2015).

Three major feminist theoretical approaches of environment, feminist political ecology, feminist environmentalism, and ecofeminism, were explored to frame this study. All these approaches theorize gender and gender relations in a specific way depending on their stances. Thus, each of these theories and approaches offers elements and insights useful for the analysis of my thesis. More specifically, the three theories provide my thesis with the necessary tools for examining the relationship between women and environmental degradation in Bangladesh. Therefore, the thesis aims to apply these theoretical approaches to provide a feminist analysis as a means to understanding women's experiences of the environment in Bangladesh, particularly in relation to climate change.

Within the broader school of political ecology, *feminist political ecology* elaborates a new and useful conceptual context. It emphasizes the gendered material understanding of the environment, the nature of resource access and control, and the relationship between local struggles and global environmental contexts (Rocheleau and Edmunds, 1997; Leach, 2007). It focuses on the unequal distribution of access to and control over resources where women have a disproportionate share (Rocheleau et al., 1996; Sachs, 1996). Thomas-Slayter et al. (1996, p. 287) state that "feminist political ecology brings into a single framework a feminist perspective combined with analysis of ecological, economic, and political power relations." Thus, feminist political ecology extends the scope of political ecology to examine the decision-making processes, as well as the social, political, and economic context that shapes environmental policies and practices from a gender perspective (Rocheleau et al., 1996). Furthermore, the authors state that,

> Feminist political ecology treats gender as a critical variable in shaping resource access and control, interacting with class, caste, race, culture, and ethnicity to shape processes of ecological change, the struggle of men and women to sustain ecologically viable livelihoods, and the prospects of any community for "sustainable development." (1996, p. 4)

Indeed, according to Hovorka (2006, p. 209), "Feminist Political Ecology aims at analyzing gendered experiences of and responses to environmental and political-economic change that brings with it changing livelihoods, landscapes, property regimes, and social relations." Hence, feminist political ecology does not only focus on environmental problems but also offers potential solutions. Feminist political ecology inspires a focus on "the importance of gendered human agency and social structure in shaping pivotal environmental policies and decisions" (Thomas-Slayter et al., 1996, p. 289). Nightingale (2006, p. 169) points out that feminist political ecology analyses gender relations in the production of knowledge, resource development, and socio-political processes. These all provide a significant difference in the opportunities and challenges presented to men and women in the context of environmental change and development. Hence, feminist political ecology deals with three key themes. The first theme is that of *gendered knowledge* which "encompasses the creation, maintenance and protection of a healthy environment at home, at work and in regional ecosystems" (Rocheleau et al., 1996, p. 4). The second theme is *gendered environment rights and responsibilities,* which considers "property, resources, space and all the variations of legal and customary rights that are 'gendered' " (Rocheleau et al.,

1996, pp. 4–5). The final theme of *gendered environmental politics and grassroots activism* highlights the collective struggle of women over "natural resource and environmental issues…contributing to a redefinition of their identities" (Rocheleau et al., 1996, pp. 4–5). The importance of feminist political ecology theory lies in its exploration of women's knowledge and experience within dominant and unequal patriarchal structures, particularly as applied to environmental issues such as climate change. Alston (2015, p. 20) argues that feminist political ecology emphasizes and focuses more on gendered roles, women's agencies, and networks for influencing sustainable climate change policies. Therefore, it is relevant to connect women and climate change adaptation within the gendered social structure of a country like Bangladesh.

Ecofeminism is considered one of the foundations of feminism and activism in relation to environmental issues (Christensen et al., 2009). Ecofeminism emerged in the late 1970s, highlighting the link between gender inequality and environmental sustainability, and quickly developing as a movement (Buckingham, 2004). Ecofeminists' arguments are underpinned by the idea that women and nature have a very specific and significant relationship, and that environmental degradation contributes to women's repression and exploitation (Merchant, 1992). The main contention of ecofeminism is that patriarchal power structures and processes of capital accumulation treat women and natural resources similarly so that both are hierarchically controlled and exploited (Christensen et al., 2009; Leach, 2007). As King (1989) proposes:

> There is no natural hierarchy, but human hierarchy is projected onto nature and used to justify social domination. Ecofeminism draws on feminist theory which asserts that the domination of women was the original domination in human society from which all other hierarchies flow. (1989, p. 24)

Ecofeminists have established gender as a visible social construct in analyzing environmental problems (Griffin, 1997, p. 217). Shiva (1989) explains the concept further by discussing how development, as a post-colonial concept of a market economy based on resource exploitation, was imposed on the third world by western economies. Shiva (1989, p. xvi) discusses this in terms of indigenous people and their relationship to nature in the Indian context. The author (Shiva, 1989, p. 46) claims that women have a special connection to the environment through their life experiences in both North and South. It is also argued that women's role in subsistence economies was to produce "wealth in partnership with nature" and become "experts in their own right of holistic and ecological knowledge of nature's processes" (Shiva, 1989, p. 72). The theory also argues that women have a positive relationship with nature due to their biological attributes, which in turn reinforces the idea that women are nature (Jackson, 1993; Shiva, 1993). Ecofeminists embrace the idea that women inherently have a better understanding about nature and knowledge of environmental protection because of their closeness to nature (Mies and Shiva, 2014). This form of ecofeminism is grounded in the idea that the domination of women is linked to environmental destruction in a patriarchal system. For example, the link between gender and the environment in Asia was largely stimulated by the narratives of rural and indigenous women saving trees and protesting commercial loggers by protecting forests and forest-based livelihood (Shiva, 1989).

Southern ecofeminists claim that rural women of the south are the natural caretakers of the environment, those who take care of the earth and its resources for the survival of future generations (Dankelman and Davidson, 1988; Rodda, 1991; Shiva, 1989). Indeed, Shiva (1989, p. 42) contends that "rural indigenous women are the original givers of life and are therefore the rightful caretakers of nature." Going a step further, Gaard (2015, p. 20) notes the paradox: although women are the producers of most of the world's food, it is mostly women and children who go hungry. Thus, ecofeminism provides my thesis with important insights for examining the relationship between rural Bangladeshi women and the environmental degradation they experience because of climate change.

Feminist environmentalism evolved as a direct critique to ecofeminism's spiritual and biological explanation of women and nature (Agarwal, 1992; Buckingham, 2004; Christensen et al., 2009; Seager, 1993). Instead, feminist environmental theory is more concerned with a structural analysis such as "women's lived material relationship with nature" (Agarwal, 1992, p. 151). Like feminist political ecology, it suggests that women are more adversely affected by environmental degradation because of the universal phenomenon of the gender division of labor and gender power relations (Agarwal, 1998, 2001b; Resurrección, 2013). According to Agarwal (1998, p. 198) "the link between women and the environment can be seen as structured by a given gender and class (caste/race), organization of production, reproduction, and distribution." These ideas are like those of feminist political ecology. However, in this case more attention is paid to men and women's distinctive roles, responsibilities and knowledge which shape gender-differentiated interests in natural resource management (Resurrección and Elmhirst, 2008). Agarwal (1992) argues that women's relationship with nature is neither inherent, nor closely connected. There are gendered interests in particular resources and ecological processes due to the clear distinction between daily work and responsibilities among women and men. She focuses more closely on the gendered relation with nature and from there she explains the differences between men's and women's experiences and knowledge. In a similar fashion Nightingale (2006, p. 168) emphasizes the socially constructed aspect of women's predicament, stating that "the material conditions of people's lives are complicit in producing particular environmental problems which place extra burdens on women who are responsible for the subsistence needs of their families."

Although an ecofeminist like Shiva claims that the Chipko Movement in India is an instance of ecofeminism, feminist environmentalists like Agarwal (1997b) and Rangan (2000) revisit the gender politics behind it. They observe institutional and local politics as the key driving factors in organizing a movement, which often involved the local community and in the above-mentioned case, women were at the frontier of the protest. In South Asia, agriculture is a male-dominated sector, although women also play a very significant role, which gives them some informal rights and control over production. However, in many areas, women have lost control over agricultural production due to the introduction of cash economy (Kabir, 2012, p. 70). In such contexts, a number of women's protests are conceived in many countries in South Asia as saving both their livelihood and nature for family survival (Agarwal, 1992). Women's exclusion from resources and the adverse impacts from environmental degradation that they experience often motivate their involvement in grassroots protests "to supplement their [missing] income" and survival (Agarwal, 1994, p. 456). Thus, the feminist environmentalist viewpoint is reflected in my thesis' exploration of the survival or coping strategies of women within persistently marginalizing class and gender relations which confine them to unequal access to and control over resources.

More recently, a growing number of feminist-informed research approaches (for instance) have examined the daily experiences of women in the context of climate change.[1] The overarching theme of these works is that the social dimension of climate change is not gender neutral (Terry, 2009). Rather, they claim that climate change has gender-differentiated causes and effects while examining the most adversely affected group by the anthropogenic climate change (Macgregor, 2009, p. 130). Such research often draws on the empirical analysis of the gender division of labor, the social construction of gender roles and responsibilities that

---

[1.] See MacGregor (2009); McCright (2010); Banerjee and Bell (2007); Terry (2009); Selam (2006); Martin (2006).

influence the access to natural resources and women's daily experiences with degradations linked to climate change (Hawkins and Ojeda, 2011).

The impacts of climate change must link the environmental aspects to the historical, social, economic, and political fabric of society (Dankelman, 2002; Denton, 2002). In many South Asian countries, women lack power, resources, information and have less geographical mobility compared with their male counterparts. All of these factors are the outcome of socially constructed gender roles (Agarwal, 2010, p. 103). It follows that it is women who often experience added exposure when climate-related environmental degradation occurs (Agarwal, 2009). This tells that feminist environmental theories are extremely useful in analyzing the link between gender and climate change.

Research Approach

This was a qualitative study that focuses on a deeper understanding and examination of current any phenomenon or issue. The main strength of a qualitative study is that it concentrates on a smaller scale but captures deeper insights than the large samples that quantitative studies use (Griffin, 2004; Rowley, 2002). The study was about the potential climate change impacts on affected communities in Bangladesh and the different adaptation initiatives that have been undertaken. As a qualitative study "case study" approach was chosen to achieve the objectives of the study because case studies are more appropriate for qualitative research and qualitative data (Rose et al., 2014). From Yin's (2014, p. 16) viewpoint, case studies are the best approach for understanding complex social phenomena, particularly real-life events. He explained a case study as an "empirical inquiry that investigates a contemporary phenomenon (the 'case') in depth and within its real-life context, especially when the boundaries between phenomenon and context are not clearly evident." King et al. (1994) also state that this type of research approach is applicable in the social sciences where particular events, institutions, locations, issues, legislation, or policies are studied. Yin (1994, p. 1) notes that "case studies are the preferred strategy when 'how' or 'why' questions are being posed, and when the focus is on a contemporary phenomenon." Generally, "how," "what," and "why" questions are the foundation of qualitative research including exploratory, descriptive, or explanatory research and a case study approach supports the "deeper and more detailed investigation" that is needed to answer these queries (Rowley, 2002, p. 17).

The purpose of the study was to develop a better understanding of climate change's impacts on selected communities, gender-differentiated vulnerabilities, and women's coping strategies in the four different climate change-affected areas of Bangladesh. In addition, it examines women's roles and how are they are included or excluded in different climate change adaptation programs and policies. This requires an in-depth inquiry. The case study approach is hence appropriate for an extensive description of this real context, allowing observations of its complexity and diversity: "case study research can also facilitate a holistic perspective on causality because it treats the case as a specific whole" (Rose et al., 2014, p. 3). The case study method also allows the inclusion of many social units or cases within a single case study using a variety of data collection techniques (Yin, 2014, p. 18). Liberman (2005, p. 435) describes the approach of the study as "Nested Analysis." Therefore, this thesis took the opportunity to undertake a nested analysis of multiple adaptation programs within the single case of Bangladesh.

Four CCA programs/fields as units of analysis for the case study of Bangladesh based on some frequent and common climate-induced hazards and the programs/projects dealing with these problems. The selected cases for this study were the three main climate-induced hazards of drought, cyclone, and landslides in the northern, southern, and south-eastern parts of Bangladesh respectively. Finally, another local indigenous flood adaptation practice was chosen in the central area of Bangladesh as an informal area of adaptation. Government and its development partners carry out mainly formal adaptation programs, whereas local communities themselves initiate many local-level autonomous coping practices based on their traditional knowledge base. Therefore, these four major climate-induced hazards and adaptation practices were selected to achieve a broader view of the overall topic. Although a case study cannot generalize findings like survey or statistical analysis can, it offers analytical generalization through multiple cases (Yin, 2003, pp. 47–48). Rowley (2002, p. 20) argues that "in analytic generalization, each case is viewed as an experiment, and not a case within an experiment. The greater the number of case studies that show replication the greater the rigor with which a theory has been established." Therefore, these four programs in line with the case study methodology were selected for the study. The main considerations for selecting the programs are: (a) geo-social conditions of the areas, (b) affected groups, (c) types of vulnerabilities, (d) adaptation or coping practices, (e) program-implementing organizations, and (f) local stakeholders.

Selection of Cases

Bangladesh is in many ways a typical example of many other underdeveloped South Asian countries confronting similar kinds of climate change impacts. In a country like Bangladesh, the social vulnerabilities of climate change are strongly connected with its poverty and gender inequality. Its under-resourced socio-economic sectors and unequal gender relations offer similarities with many countries all over the world. It is thus quite possible to apply the findings of this study to other developing countries in considering the future way forward.

Map 1 presents the locations of the cases selected for the study in Bangladesh.

Map 1: Locations of the Programs Chosen for the Study in Bangladesh

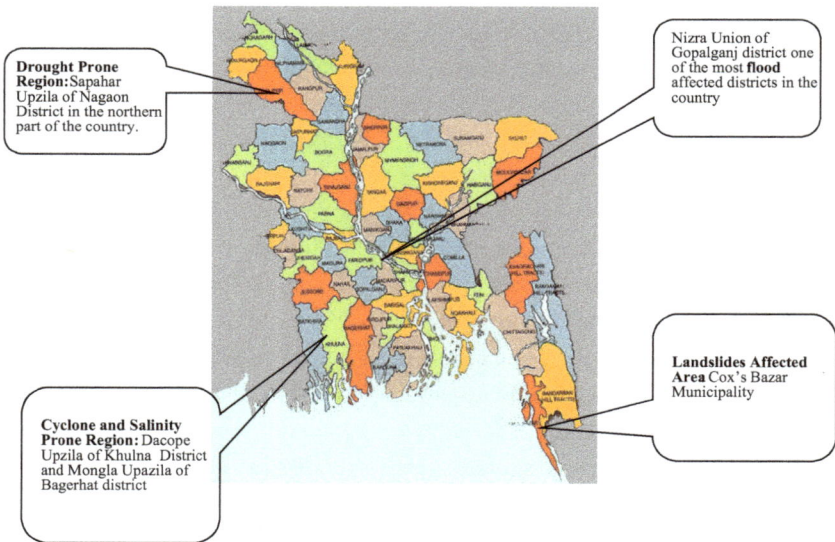

Drought Prone Region: Sapahar Upzila of Nagaon District in the northern part of the country.

Nizra Union of Gopalganj district one of the most **flood** affected districts in the country

Landslides Affected Area Cox's Bazar Municipality

Cyclone and Salinity Prone Region: Dacope Upzila of Khulna District and Mongla Upazila of Bagerhat district

Bangladesh with District Administrative Boundary
Source: https://en.m.wikipedia.org/wiki/File:BD_Map_admin.svg.

The selected fields are chosen from the southern, northern, south-eastern, and central parts of Bangladesh based on cyclone- and salinity-prone areas, drought-prone areas, landslide-affected areas, and flood-prone areas, respectively. The cases were selected on the ground of earlier studies and reports documenting climate hazards and vulnerabilities. Since the study focuses on climate change, it covers most of the climate change-related major hazards in the country. Based on statistical data obtained from different sources, a program was selected related to cyclones, since it is one of the main disasters effecting almost 17 coastal districts out of the 64 districts of Bangladesh every year. Moreover, in the recent past the effects of cyclones appeared to be more prominent in terms of frequency and intensity in the coastal belt of the country, which is attributable to climate change. Prolonged high temperatures and irregular precipitation trends in the northern part of the country have resulted in frequent seasonal droughts over the past few decades; these events are also considered an impact of climate change in Bangladesh. Landslide is a relatively new phenomenon due to uneven rainfall over the last few years in the hilly districts of the country. The migrated populations who live in the hilly urban settlement are the group most affected and at risk of this hazard. As a new urban hazard, it was important to include this in this study. Different actors were considered as implementing agencies and activities in obtaining diverse information about climate change adaptation strategies. Finally, the study explored an indigenous knowledge-based practice that has been used by local people to cope with flood, which is now a common climatic phenomenon of the country. are thus very important.

Description of Fields

Field 1: Cyclone- and Salinity-Prone Area
Geographical location:
Khulna division (Southern part)
Dacope upazila (Khulna district)
Mongla upazila (Bagerhat district)
Selected program:
Cyclone Preparedness Program

Map 2: Cyclone-Affected Areas of BD

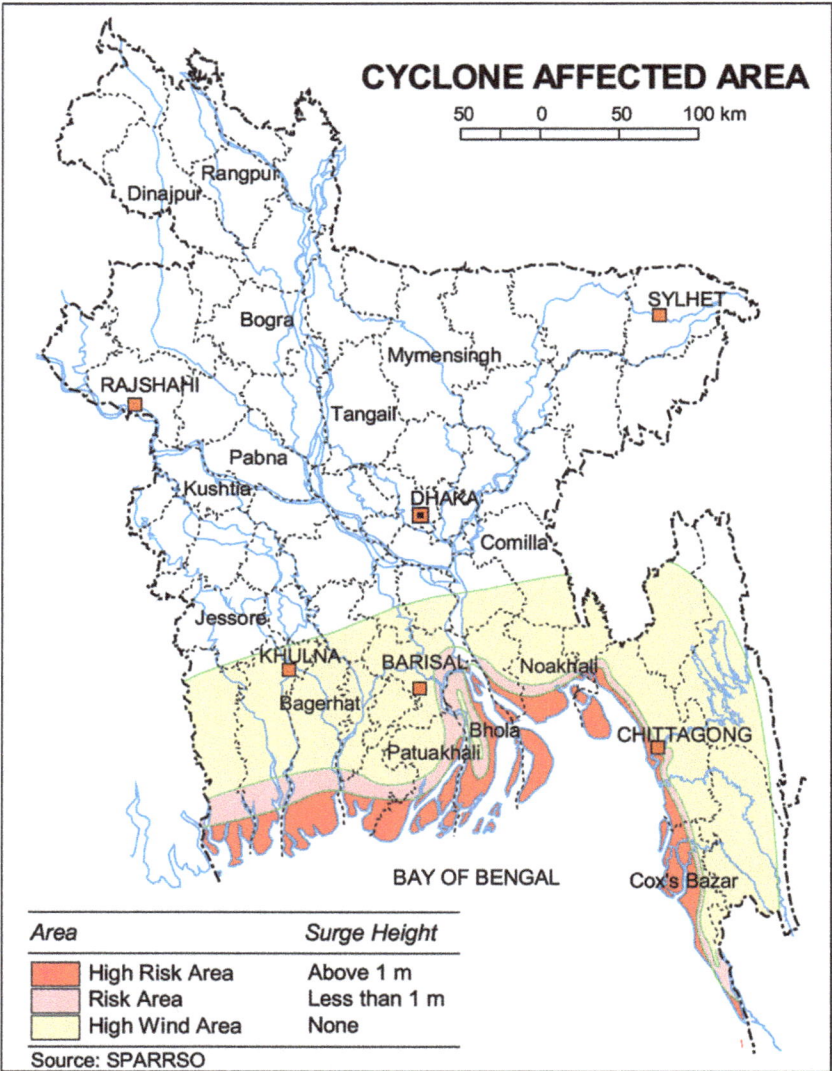

Source: Space Research and Remote Sensing Organizations;
Local Government and Engineering Department.

Map 3: Location of Khulna and Bagerhat Districts

Mongla is the second biggest seaport of the country surrounded by Rampal upazila on the north, the Bay of Bengal on the south, Morelganj and Sarankhola upazilas on the east, and Dacope upazila on the west (UDMP, 2014a, p. 2). The total land area of upazila is 1,461.20 sq. km; out of that the Sundarbans[2] holds 1,083 sq. km (UDMP,[3] 2014a, p. 1). It has 32,383 households and a total population of 137,947, of which males make up 54.73 percent and females 45.27 percent (BBS, 2022a). The average literacy rate of the population is 42.8 percent (BBS, 2011). Shrimp cultivation and agriculture are the main sources of income and economic activities of these areas (UDMP, 2014a, p. 2). The livelihood of a number of communities depends on the natural resources of the local mangrove forest Sundarbans. About 13 local, national, and international NGOs are working in Mongla, mainly carrying out microcredit, education, health, water and sanitation, and development awareness activities; in addition, these organizations provide the disaster risk reduction and climate change adaptation support for the community.[4]

Dacope upazila is surrounded by Batiaghata upazila on the north, Pashur River on the south, Rampal and Mongla upazilas on the east, and Paikgachha and Koyra upazilas on the west (UDMP, 2014b, p. 2). The total land area of this upazila is 991.98 sq. km, with the Sundarbans holding 1,283 sq. km and hosting 29,600 households (UDMP, 2014b, p. 4). The total population is 158,309, of which males comprise 50.75 percent and females 49.25 percent; the average literacy rate is 37.6 percent (BBS, 2022a). Agriculture is the main economic activity of the area, using up a total of 18,657 ha of land. In addition, prawn cultivation and fishing is the source of income for some inhabitants, while a number of people also maintain their livelihood by relying on the natural resources of the local mangrove forest Sundarbans. About 29 local, national, and international NGOs are carrying out development activities in Mongla, which include microcredit, education, health, water and sanitation, and awareness building of development

---

[2] According to Rahman and Asaduzzaman, "Sundarban is the largest mangrove wetland in the world. It covers an area of about 1mha, of which 60% is located in Bangladesh and the remaining western portion, comprising 40%, lies in India. They protect our coast from heavy wind, tidal waves, coastal erosion and sea water intrusion, generate substantial quantities of fishery resources and provide many useful forestry products" (Rahman and Asaduzzaman, 2010, p. 35).

[3] Upazila Disaster Management Plan, Mongla, Bagerhat.

[4] Mongla upazila social welfare officer, personal communication, September 10, 2013.

activities; some organizations are involved in disaster risk reduction and climate change adaptation activities.[5]

Mongla and Dacope are the two southern sub-districts (upazilas)[6] of Bangladesh under Bagerhat and Khulna districts respectively. Both upazilas are situated on the bank of the local river Pashur. The areas were chosen because they are the most cyclone- and salinity-prone areas of the country. The Sundarbans is on the south which was one of the worst affected areas during cyclones SIDR, AILA, and MOHASEN in 2007, 2009, and 2013 respectively. Within a number of disaster management and climate change adaptation programs I have selected the Cyclone Preparedness Program as the first government initiative in 1972 for cyclone preparedness with the aim of developing disaster-resilient coastal communities.

Field 2: Drought-Prone Area
Geographical location:
Rajshai division (northern part)
Sapahar upazila (Naogaon district)
Babupur and Haripur unions
Selected Program:
A livelihood-based drought adaptation program supported by Action Aid

---

[5] Dacope upazila social welfare officer, personal communication, September 15, 2013.

[6] Bangladesh has seven administrative divisions. Within these the urban local government has a single tier and the rural local government has three tiers: 64 Districts, which are divided into around 500 upazilas (sub-districts). Upazilas are subdivided again into around 4,500 union parishad. Each upazila has an elected chairman, a female vice-chairman and nine members including reserved seats for women (S. Rahman, 2012).

Map 4: Drought Map of Bangladesh

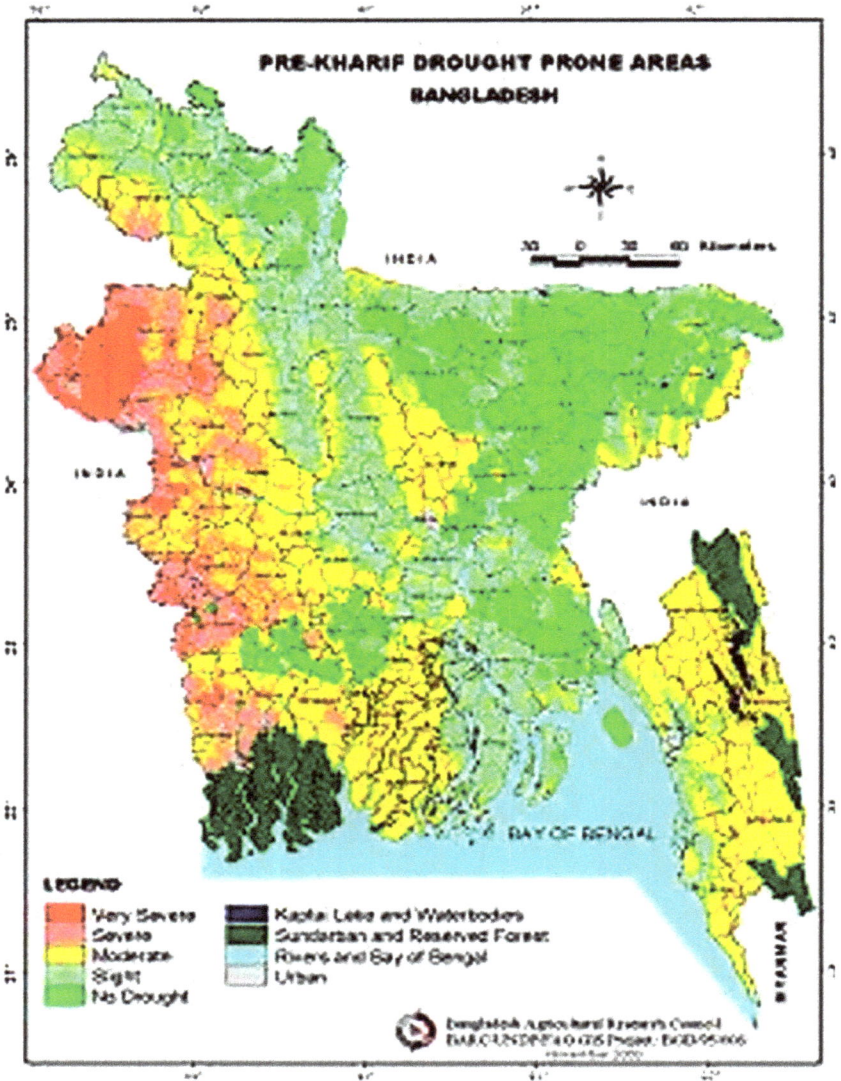

Map 5: Location of Naogaon District

Source: Local Government and Engineering Department.

Sapahar upazila is a sub-district of Naogaon district of the Rajshahi division. Sapahar upazila is surrounded by the West Bengal state of India on the north and west, Porsha upazila on the south, and Patnitala upazila on the east. The upazila has two main water bodies: the river Punarbhaba and the Jabai Beel. The total land area of Sapahar is 244.49 sq. km and it hosts 19,770 households; the total population of Sapahar upazila is 161,792 and the ratio of male-to-female population is 1:1.16 (UDMP, 2014c, p. 8). Most of the population follows Islam, though 2.01 percent of the population are ethnic minorities who follow their own traditions, culture, and religions (BBS, 2011). The percentage of literate population of Sapahar upazila is 47.1 (7+ years). Agriculture is the main occupation, involving 52.15 percent of its inhabitants, whereas the rest of the population are agricultural laborers (22.58 percent, who do not own land), wage laborers (3.07 percent), businessmen (7.14 percent), service providers (7.47 percent), and others (7.59 percent). The upazila has a total of 25,162 ha of cultivable land on which crop cultivation is allocated as follows: 62 percent grows a single crop, 29 percent a double crop, and 9 percent a triple crop (UDMP, 2014c, p. 12). Approximately 15 national, international, and local NGOs are working in this upazila providing education, health, microcredit, medical services, and education loans for their beneficiaries.[7] In addition, they are implementing large-scale community or social forestry as a part of drought adaptation programs.

Drought is a regular phenomenon in the north-west region of Bangladesh where this upazila is situated (CDMP, 2013). According to the drought map prepared by the Bangladesh Agricultural Research Council, the Naogaon district is in the first position in terms of severity ranking and Sapahar upazila is one of the most severely affected areas of the district. Both seasonal and prolonged droughts are causing serious problems for the cultivation of crops, and they create seasonal unemployment for agriculture-dependent populations. A number of adaptation initiatives have been undertaken by different actors to cope with drought impacts. Among them a program was selected which is implemented by one of the Bangladeshi Government's development partners, Action Aid Bangladesh.

Field 3: Landslide-Affected Area
  Geographical location:
  Chittagong division (south-eastern part)
  Cox's Bazar municipality (Cox's Bazar district)
  Jadipahar and Mohajer Para wards
  Selected program:
  Community-based early warning for Landslides Resiliency program

---

[7] Sapahar upazila social welfare officer, personal communication, October 15, 2013.

Figure 1: Landslide-Affected Areas

Cox's Bazar is a district of Chittagong division and one of the world's longest (120 kilometres) natural sea beaches (Hassan and Shahnewaz, 2014, p. 32). It is situated at the basin of the Bay of Bengal in the south and west; bordered by Chittagong district in the north, and Myanmar in the east. Cox's Bazaar district is comprised of islands, rivers, hills, and flat lands with an area of 2491.86 square kilometres (MDMP, 2014, p. 4). It was constituted as a municipality in 1869 and it covers an area of 6.85 square kilometres with 27 mahallas and nine wards and has a population of 51,918 (Ahammed, 2010, p. 1). Cox's Bazar is also the main seaport of Bangladesh.

Map 6: Location of Cox's Bazar District

Source: Local Government and Engineering Department.

Tourism is the major source of income in Cox's Bazar; consequently, people are involved in associated tourist activities (Hassan and Shahnewaz, 2014). Fishing and collecting seafood and sea products are also the main sources of many people's livelihoods (Ahammed, 2010). Sea products-related activities such as selling different types of oysters, snails, and pearl ornaments are mainly backed by women's home-based informal labor and are very popular businesses with tourists in seaside and city stores.[8] In addition, Cox's Bazar is also considered

---

[8.] Women affairs officer, personal communication, December 12, 2013.

one of the major aquaculture producer districts in Bangladesh, which is a major source of foreign export revenue. Cox's Bazar plays an important role in the national economy with its small-scale agriculture, marine and inland fishing, salt production, and other industrial sources (Hassan and Shahnewaz, 2014, p. 33). Consequently, rapid urbanization is prevalent here.

According to a study by CDMP (2012a), Cox's Bazar has experienced major problems with landslides over the last few years. This study (CDMP 2012a, pp. 11–12) claims that between 1999 and 2010, a total of 268 people were killed due to several landslides, and in 2007, one landslide alone killed 127 people in Chittagong. The government of Bangladesh, with the support of the Asian Disaster Preparedness Center, has initiated community-based early warning systems at two urban municipalities, Cox's Bazar and Teknaf, as a part of landslides risk mitigation and development of community resilience. This community-based adaptation program was selected because it is the first initiative that addresses landslide hazards by the government with the support of a development partner.

Field 4: Flood-Prone Area

Geographical location:
Gopalganj district (Middle part)
Nizra union (Gopalganj Sadar upazila)
Selected adaptation practice:
Floating Garden—an indigenous flood adaptation practice

Map 7: Flood Water Map of Bangladesh

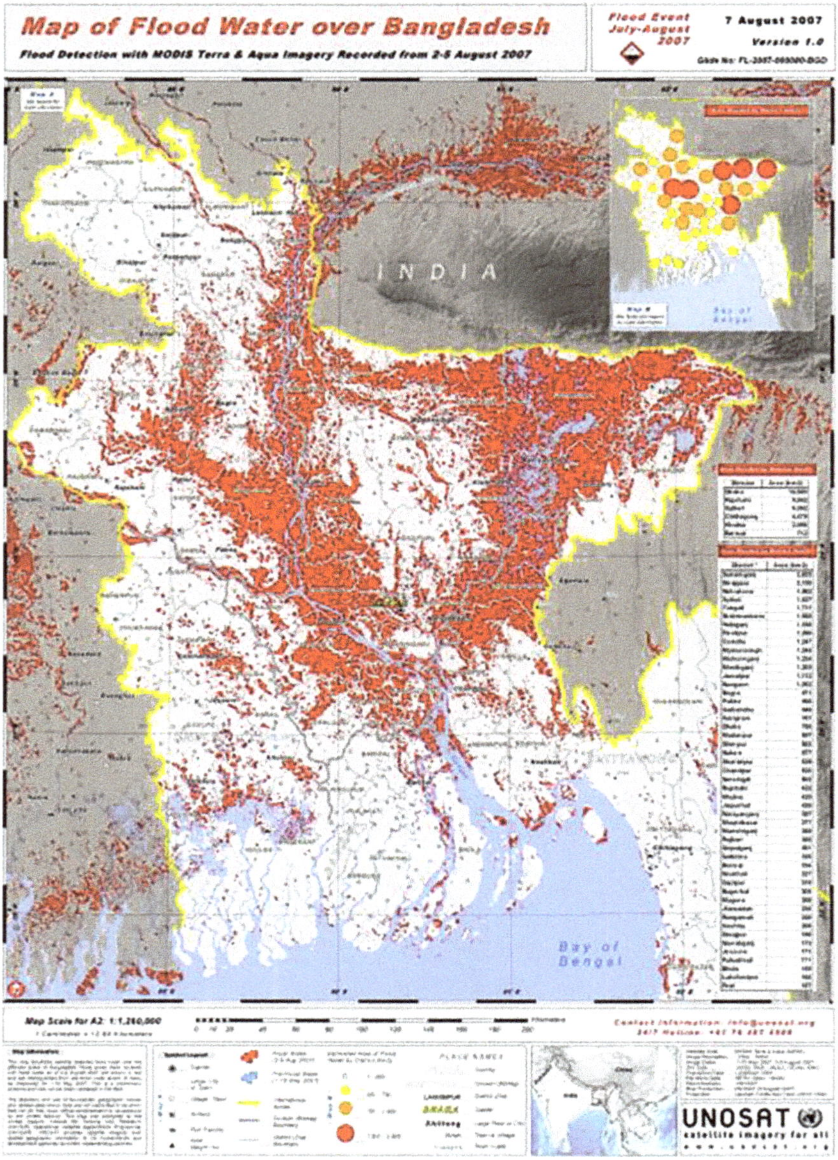

Map 8: Location Map of Gopalganj District

Sources: Space Research and Remote Sensing Organizations;
Local Government and Engineering Department.

Nizra is a union parishad[9] under Gopalganj Sadar upazila of Gopalganj district. It is situated at the bank of river Madhumati. Agriculture is the predominant economic activity of this area which produces a variety of crops such as rice, sugarcane, wheat, vegetables, spices, jute, pulses, and other minor cereals. People are also involved in non-farm activities such as small businesses, construction works, hospitality and transport in the nearby Gopalganj town, although female participation in non-farm activities is very low (UDMP, 2014d).

---

[9] Union parishad is the oldest and lowest tier of local government of Bangladesh. It has been functioning for more than a 100 years for the local development of the country. At present there are 4,480 Union parishads which have directly elected local representatives: one Chairman and nine members, including three female members (https://en.wikipedia.org/wiki/Union_councils_of_Bangladesh).

As discussed above, Bangladesh is one of the most flood-affected countries in the world, with floods occurring almost yearly in different regions. According to the flood map (CDMP, 2014c), Gopalganj is one of the most flood-prone districts. Nizra union is in the middle region of Bangladesh, located in the flood plain and in the middle of marshy land. The settlements are scattered on raised land to avoid seasonal flooding. Almost half of the year the village remains under water as the large flood plain continues to be the basin of large catchment areas across the upazila.[10] About 90 percent of the village area is not usable for normal vegetation except deep-water rice which can grow 25 cm (9.8 in.) a day to reach a length of up to 7 m (23 ft.) and survive in 4 m-deep (13 ft.) water. Since flood is a regular phenomenon in Bangladesh, people have learnt how to live with it. A number of coping strategies are practiced across the country; among those the floating garden is a unique livelihood practice, which was selected as an example of local indigenous coping practice for study.

Data Collection Methods and Selection of Participants

To achieve the objectives of the study, both primary and secondary sources were used for collecting relevant data and information. The main sources of primary data were from field observation, focus group discussions, semi-structured interviews with local people, in-depth interviews with women and interviews with key informants at the national level. Two sets of questionnaires were designed based on the research questions and aims of this study: one for the local level and the other for national-level key informants. A detailed description of the data collection process is as follows.

A total 12 FGDs were conducted with the selected communities in particular areas. These include 10 FGDs in cyclone- and salinity-impacted areas, drought-prone areas, and landslide-affected areas. Three FGDs, each comprising 10–12 participants, were arranged in each area (four FGDs were conducted in cyclone- and salinity-prone areas). One was a mixed male–female participants group and two were with female participants only. Among the female focus groups, one was with beneficiaries of the program, and another was with members of a grassroots women's organization. Alongside these, two FGDs were conducted

---

[10.] Gopalganj upazila agriculture officer, personal communication, September 20, 2013.

in the indigenous flood adaptation area: one was with both men and women and the other was with local women in a particular locality.

Two to three women were chosen from each area for in-depth interviews during the FGDs in order to prepare stories on their life experience. In total, 10 in-depth interviews were conducted with women from various regions. The women were chosen based on four factors: women who were more expressive about their problems and solutions, women who had direct disaster experiences, women who attempted to overcome the situation, and women involved in a process of changing their lives. This was purposive sampling because my intention was to look at women's individual experiences to explore their roles, indigenous knowledge and resilience in climate change adaptation and disaster management more intensively. These in-depth discussions allowed the respondents to depict their daily life experiences and raise issues about their environment, climate change, and their livelihood patterns to cope with the situation from a woman's perspective. Furthermore, they offered valuable insights into gender issues regarding vulnerability and adaptive capacity. For these in-depth interviews, it was necessary to spend an extensive period with them at their houses. I was allowed to interview them alongside their household work, as it was difficult for them to spare 4 or 5 hours for the interview.

Five interviews with local-level government officials, NGO staff, community leaders, and local government representatives were conducted from each selected area, which added up to a total of 20 interviews. For the local-level interviews the key persons were selected related to climate change adaptation at the local level such as local government representatives, heads of the local administration, officers from the DWA, and officers and related NGO personnel. This process helped to gather more practical information and provided scope for data triangulation and validation. For the national-level expert interviews, selected key players in climate change initiatives were professionals, activists, academics, practitioners, and high-level government and non-government officials. These interviews enriched the knowledge of climate change impacts and vulnerabilities, as well as adaptation strategies in Bangladesh. In particular, they helped to understand gender considerations within adaptation programs, policies and related issues. Table 5 presents a summary of the methods and number of participants of the study, while Table 6 outlines the gender segregation of the interviewees.

Secondary data related to the study were collected from various sources such as relevant government offices, international development agencies, NGOs, and libraries of research organizations. Different national and international policy documents, project documents, previous research and study reports, journal articles, maps, and census data were also used as secondary data and information sources.

Table 5: Research Methods Used to Collect Data and Information

Method	Participants	Number
Primary Data Collection		
Focus group discussion[11]	Community members (a group of 10–12 participants) One mixed group; two female groups	12 (approximately 130 participants) (three FGDs from three fields, and two FGDS in Indigenous practice) total 12 FGDs
Interviews with local program stakeholders[12]	Local-level government officials, workers of non-government organizations, community leaders, local government representatives	20 (five interviews from each field)
Field observation	Respective areas and programs	Four selected fields
Key informant interview[13]	Policy makers, government officials, non-government officials, gender and environment activists, practitioners, academicians	20 KI from National and International experts
In-depth interview[14]	Women directly involving in adaptation programs or individual response	10 (2/3 women from each area)
Secondary Data Collection		
Documentary research, institutional policy mapping, and program documents analysis		

---

[11] Women's groups henceforth stated as FGD.WG and mixed group as FGD.MG.

[12] Interviews with program stakeholders henceforth stated as LII (Local Informant Interviewee).

[13] National level key informant interview stated as KII.

[14] In-depth interview with individual women stated as IDI.

Table 6: Gender Segregation of the Interviewees

Type of Interviewee	No. of Female Interviewees	No. of Male Interviewees	Total
National-level key Informants	7	13	20
Local-level key Informants	6	14	20
In-depth interview	10		10
Total	**23**	**27**	**50**

Note: more women were in the FGDs compared to male participants; of a total of 130 participants, 90 were women and 40 were men.

Analysis

As "interpretative and subjective research" (Lacey and Donna, 2007, p. 6), qualitative data analysis requires the "subjective interpretation of the content of the text data using the systematic classification process of coding and identifying themes or patterns" (Hsieh and Shannon, 2005, p. 1278). Therefore, it is critical to summarize, classify and highlight important themes or ideas for data analysis of qualitative research. Bachman and Schutt (2014, p. 263) argue that "conceptualizing begins with a simple observation that is interpreted directly, 'pulled apart', and then put back together more meaningfully." There are software packages or manual methods to analyze qualitative data. Manual analyses were undertaken by following the major steps of qualitative data analysis which include coding, identification of themes, recoding, development of categories, identification of relationships between categories and refinement of themes (see Lacey and Donna, 2007, p. 7). As my data size was not too large and hence manageable, manual analysis was considered appropriate (see Basit, 2003, p. 152). The questionnaires and talking points were developed in English and then translated to Bangla, which is the national and common language of Bangladeshi people. Before conducting all interviews and FGDs, verbal and written consent was collected from the participants. The interviews were tape recorded, verbatim transcriptions were prepared from the recordings and then the data were coded. Most interviews were in Bangla; only direct quotes were translated into English to use them in findings and analysis. Summarized transcribed data were merged under the thematic areas. These themes were developed on the basis of the objectives, research questions and the theoretical framework of the study. The themes include climate change in Bangladesh, visible impacts of climate change, socio-economic vulnerabilities, gender division of labor, women's roles, gendered knowledge, gender perceptions, and gender mainstreaming. Finally, a thematic analysis was completed based on the theoretical framework of the study.

CHAPTER 3

Gender Relations and Climate Change: Suffering of Women in Bangladesh

What the societies have in common are the practice of rigid gender segregation, specific forms of family and kinship and a powerful ideology linking family honour to female virtue. Men are entrusted with safeguarding family honour through their control over female members; they are backed by complex social arrangements which ensure the protection—and dependence—of women.

(Kabeer, 1988)

Bangladesh is a traditional patriarchal society, where males play a dominant role within the family, the community, and society as a whole. This situation is pervasive within states, political institutions, and legal systems as the consequence of deeply rooted unequal gender relations. According to Kabeer and Mahmud (2004, p. 94) in Bangladesh there is a strict patriarchal structure which includes "the practice of female seclusion, patrilineal principles of descent and inheritance [and] patrilocal principles of marriage." Another study by The United Nations Children's Fund (UNICEF) (2010) argues that the mobility of Bangladeshi women is controlled, and male family members often make the decisions. In particular, economic decisions such as women's health and employment-related issues are usually determined by their husbands. Due to prevalent cultural and socio-economic conditions women experience structural discrimination such as access to and control over resources, less opportunity for employment and under-representation in the political sphere (Ahmed and Maitra, 2010, p. 83).

Currently, in Bangladesh, the male-to-female ratio is 49.51:50.49 (Bangladesh Bureau of Statistics [BBS], 2022a), which indicates an increasing female population, since in the earlier census (2011) the ratio was 50.1:49.9. BBS provides a statistical overview of the women's position in Bangladesh. Some important indicators selected for understanding the gender relations in Bangladesh are presented in the following table.

Table 7: Selected Indicators of Gender Relation in Bangladesh

Indicator	Gender Segregation	Percentage	Source
Labor force participation (15+)	Women	42.7	Labour Force Survey, BBS (2022c)
	Men	80.0	
Employed population	Women	24.6	Labour Force Survey, BBS (2022c)
	Men	45.6	
Informal employment (non-agriculture)	Women	34.5	Labour Force Survey, BBS (2022c)
	Men	11.8	
Unpaid family worker	Women	3.1 (million)	Labour Force Survey, BBS (2022c)
	Men	1.7 (million)	
Literacy rate	Women	72.3	HIES, 2022
	Men	75.8	
Population (aged 15–24 years) not in education, employment, and training (NEET)	Women	1.9	Population and Housing Census 2022
	Men	8.8	
Population (aged 15 years and above) having an account in a financial institution (bank/insurance/micro-credit/post office etc.)	Women	19.8	Population and Housing Census 2022
	Men	28.5	
Number elected female members in the national parliament	Women	19	Bangladesh Parliament, 2024
	Men	281	

The statistics exhibit a large gender disparity in relation to women's economic status both for urban and rural areas. However, the unemployment status of women does not mean that women do not engage in any type of economic activities. According to Kabeer and Mahmud (2004, p. 94) this scenario reinforces women's restricted mobility in the public domain as they either work as unpaid family laborers or engage in informal work within the home. The labor market in Bangladesh is very male dominated with women mostly relegated to work in the informal sector. Women also receive lower wages than men in paid employment sectors in both rural and urban areas and the status of employment, occupation and hours of work are determined by males (Ahmed and Maitra, 2010, p. 85). A study conducted by Oxfam and Somasthe (Moni, 2016)[1] claims that despite not being recognized as farmers, 61.1 percent of the female labor force is involved in agriculture, which is more than their participation in the ready-made garments (RMG) sector. This contradicts a previous claim that the majority of female labor engages in the ready-made garments sector and shows that women's labor force participation in agriculture is an under-represented phenomenon. However, women's involvement in some formal sectors (public and private) such as ready-made garments, shrimp processing, cosmetics, shoes, and pharmaceutical industries is significant, and women's economic participation rate has increased from 36 to 42 percent during the period 2010–2022 (BBS, 2022c). Among those in the RMG sector, about 90 percent of workers are women, and this sector has played a significant role in the country's economic success over the last two decades (Haque et al., 2020).

In Bangladesh, households are mainly headed and controlled by men (87.4 percent) and only 12.6 percent of households are led by women (HIES, 2022). The proportion of female-headed households has increased more in urban areas than rural areas since the last census. Interestingly, female-headed households experience less poverty (26.6 percent) than male-headed households (32.1 percent), although the female-headed household's monthly average income is lower than that of the male-headed household (BBS, 2011, p. xxii). Women usually adopt many strategies to maintain household food security and statistics show that 1.9 percent of women in rural areas and 1 percent in urban areas often skip meals each month (National Institute of Population Research and Training [NIOPORT], 2013). In Bangladesh, discriminatory practices and rules prevail in access to assets and distribution of property to women; they only own 3.5 percent

[1] A report published in the daily newspaper *Prothom Alo*, January 14, 2016.

of agricultural lands (Scalise, 2009, p. 32). Neither Muslim nor Hindu women of Bangladesh enjoy equal rights in inheritance of land or property (Karim, 2013, p. 161). Women's lower economic status and subordinate position results in a high prevalence of unattended home births; the high birth rate among adolescent girls and malnourishment contribute to the high maternal mortality rate; and one in every 51 women has a risk of dying during childbirth within her reproductive life span (UNICEF, 2010, p. 3). From 2000 to 2022, the maternal mortality ratio (MMR) in Bangladesh declined by 38 percent—from 441 deaths to 156 deaths per 100,000 live births (Bangladesh Sample Vital Statistics, 2022)

Despite such constraints, Bangladeshi women have experienced some positive achievements. Women's life expectancy has increased within the last 40 years from 54.3 to 74.3 years, which is higher than men (BBS, 2022a). Bangladesh is one of the countries that have achieved the first of eight millennium development goals of reducing extreme poverty rates from 58 to 29 percent between 1991 and 2012, before the targeted period, and the estimated ratio for 2015 is 24.8 percent (General Economics Division [GED], 2015, p. 9). Maternal health has improved, and the child mortality rate also has decreased significantly (from 151/1,000 to 41/1,000) within the same period from 1991 to 2013 (GED, 2015, p. 10). Bangladesh has also progressed in providing education for girls and now girls outnumber boys in primary school enrolment (GED, 2015, p. 9). The net attendance rates in secondary and tertiary education are still quite low, however improving at the secondary level 47.8 percent are girls and 52.7 percent boys and at the tertiary level, there are six girls for every 10 boys (BBS, 2018). The achievements in the health and education sectors are strongly related to chang-ing gender relations and an increasing awareness level for women (Hossain and Kabeer, 2004). Currently, Bangladesh's position in the global gender gap index is 59th globally and top in South Asia which is a significant progress within the last 8 years. In 2007, its rank was 100, and within South Asian countries, its current position is at the top (World Economic Form [WEF], 2023).

Despite the persisting inequalities, Bangladeshi women have historically shown great resilience and courage in confronting social, economic, political, and envi-ronmental problems. Women's active participation in advancing civil and political rights is an important factor in their overall advancement (Azim, 2010, p. 263). For example, thousands of women actively participated in the liberation war in 1971 along with men and their sacrifice and supportive role played a significant part in achieving the victory (M. Begum, 2012). After independence (1972) the women's equality movement in Bangladesh gained momentum through the influence of various organizations including NGOs, women's groups and other civil society organizations (Mohsin, 2010, pp. 17–19). In recent years, a large number of NGOs have played a vital role in bringing women into public spaces in rural Bangladesh: the microcredit sector is one such initiative. According to Islam (2015, p. 48), Bangladesh's microcredit sector had received global attention for "the speed at which it grew to its present size and prominence." Rural women of Bangladesh are the main drivers of the microfinance sector. This has helped them to improve their household well-being along with facilitating economic empowerment. In effect, many NGOs have accessed the social fabric to bring qualitative change in the life of rural women in Bangladesh (Tanjeela, 2008, p. 81).

The Constitution of Bangladesh guarantees equal rights of women in every sphere of their life and even provides for special affirmative measures to promote equality.[2] To promote women's development the Government of Bangladesh has put in place measures which include increasing girls' equal access to education, creating opportunities for women's employment, increasing women's political representation, and enacting new laws and reformation of others for women[3] (GED, 2015, p. 10). Among these, women's participation at the local political domain is a particularly important step. The provision of three elected seats for women in the local governmental bodies is a significant and encouraging effort to increase women's political participation in Bangladesh (Tanjeela, 2008). However, initially during 1997, there was a lack of women's presence and interest to participate actively in the election. The scenario has changed and at present the inclusion of a female vice-chairman post at upazila Parishad (second tier of local government) has improved the situation positively (S. Rahman, 2012). Consequently, more women are being encouraged to engage in the formal power structure at both union parishad and upazila level, which is a positive aspect for the advancement of local women. Indeed, women's representation and participation in politics are the prerequisites for ensuring women's empowerment by incorporating them in decision-making bodies (Mohsin, 2010, p. 21). Women's participation in local government bodies has

---

[2] The Constitution of Bangladesh was formulated in 1972 soon after its independence. The Constitution offers equal right to women which include: participation of women in national life (Article 10); equal opportunity for all citizens (Article 19(1) subsection 2); equality before law (Article 27); equal opportunity in public employment (Article 29); participation in parliament (Article 65) (LPAD, 2010).

3. Bangladesh is now implementing the Fourth National Women's Development Policy, which was put in practice in 2011. A vast range of activities were incorporated to expedite the development of women in Bangladesh.

resulted in a significant number of women becoming involved in local politics as well as local development activities.

Bangladeshi women as a socially disadvantaged group are confronting serious negative effects through their daily life experiences. Critical gender-specific problems in the era of climate change and environmental degradation in Bangladesh are discussed below.

The Burden of the Gender Division of Labor

Bangladesh is a traditional country where gender-differentiated roles are deeply entrenched in its social structure. As a result of a strong gender division of labor, men do not usually perform household activities. Therefore, that burden ultimately falls upon women, who are accustomed to the situation. A group of women shared their views on the gendered household division of labor:

> How can we ask men to cook, clean, wash and take care of the children since these are our duties? They will be humiliated in front of other people if they do these household tasks because men and women have separate duties. It does not matter how much burden falls on our shoulders. Men do the hard labor in the agricultural fields and, to earn money, they do jobs that women cannot do. (FGD.WG2, 2013)

The gender division of labor makes women responsible for the provision of the household's food and consequently for other related activities such as collecting water and firewood and arranging food grains.[4] A woman from Mongla upazila expresses it this way:

> As a mother, it is not possible to accept that my children might starve. So, I need to arrange food at any cost. I collect foodstuff such as leaves and root vegetables from fields, sometimes I catch small fishes from the river or work in the well-off neighbor's house to provide food for my family members. (IDI.3, 2014)

---

[4] Neelormi and Ahmed (2009) found that women and adolescent girls in the coastal areas are affected adversely by climate change, since they are responsible for ensuring water and food for the family.

Moreover, household responsibilities and caregiver roles mean that women have limited mobility, while physical safety issues constrain their coping strategies (Azad and Pritchard, 2023). The situation is aggravated by the effects of climate change. The following statement provides an insight into how gender roles define women's choices and force them to make significant sacrifices. A local woman from Sutarkhali union of Dacope upazila shares her personal experiences:

> My daughter had to stop her schooling because she needed to help me to carry water and there was no other alternative. She is not the only one who had to drop out from school: there are many girls like her in our area who are the main helpers of their mothers to collect water for their households. (FGD.MG2, 2013)

Salinity intrusion, especially contamination of drinking water sources in coastal belts, appears to be the most important concern for the coastal areas, especially for women (see CCC, 2009a; Women's Environment and Development Organization [WEDO], 2008). The respondents of my study also feel strongly about the changes to the biophysical environment that they are personally experiencing in their everyday lives.

Safety and Security Stress

The dichotomy between private and public life plays an important role in women's lives in Bangladesh. For this reason, women are often subjected to men's insensitivity and their patronizing attitudes, especially in public spaces. Moreover, women's safety and security become a significant issue during natural disasters (see Nasreen, 2008b; Rashid and Michaud, 2000). Alston (2015, p. 120) highlights Bangladeshi women and adolescent girls' safety and privacy-related issues as an important consequence of natural disasters. A statement from one of the local-level informants in Dacope upazila, who is directly involved in the local-level disaster preparedness and climate change adaptation-related activities, resonates similar concerns:

> *It is a big challenge for us that women are not willing to go to cyclone shelters because they do not feel comfortable in common public places and always fear loss of dignity. Ordinary local women do not have much mobility in our area.*

They seldom come out in public places, and this makes them more vulnerable
during a disaster as they need to step out of their home. (LI.2 2013)

These hostile situations discourage women from taking refuge in cyclone shelters
or evacuation centers which leads to increased casualties among them. Moreover,
previous histories of disasters provide evidence of women's vulnerabilities due
to their gender identity.

Falling into the Poverty Trap

Climate-induced migration has gender-differentiated consequences (Gray and
Mueller, 2012), particularly for poor households. Women are "trapped" in poverty
when husbands or other male family members migrate or leave behind them the
burden of unpaid loans; they also have fewer options to migrate (Beddington,
2011; Kartiki, 2011). This study also found that many men from every locality
left the village in search of a new livelihood in nearby districts or cities. When
women are left behind, they are burdened with household responsibilities and
as a result, they are always at risk of falling into more poverty, as described
by several participants. Women from Babupur union of Sapahar district have
commented on the changing social scenarios:

> Due to loss of crop production and livelihood, many males from our area started
> to move to town or other districts to earn money for their families' expenditure.
> Unfortunately, not all of them come back home or send money. Here you will find
> many families are struggling to survive due to the absence of the husband or male
> members, but women cannot leave their family or children. (FGD.WG3, 2013)

Effect on Health and Well-being

A recent study reveals that women in salinity prone areas are suffering from high
levels of anemia and blood pressure which increases health issues, particularly for
pregnant women (Morol, 2015, pp. 1–4).[5] In Bangladesh, as in many patriarchal
societies, when families experience an economic crisis women's health expenditure is the first cost to be cut (Begum, 1997). The situation of women in Dacope

---

[5.] The report was published in *Prothom Alo* (a daily newspaper of Bangladesh) on November 17, 2015.

upazila is even more severe. Sometimes they do not have the option of visiting a doctor, although they frequently suffer from urinary and reproductive-related diseases because of the water crisis. During and after disasters women and adolescent girls face major problems regarding their health due to the collapse of health and sanitation systems (see WEDO, 2008). Faced with this situation, members from a local women's group named "Nari Bikash Kendra" of Mongla upazila shared their experiences:

> We cannot use salt water for our domestic work, even for washing clothes. Most of the time, we cannot clean our body properly due to the shortage of water. We face more difficulties during our menstrual periods. Many of us have problems such as vaginal and urinal infections, as well as miscarriages; these issues are making our lives miserable. You know women have many different and special types of needs and requirements, which are rarely taken into consideration. We are facing some health problems that we cannot share with others. (FDG. WG1, 2014)

The situation for women who have migrated to urban slums is even more diffi-cult. In particular, adult females have a double or triple probability of reporting illnesses related to reproductive health emergencies due to poor nutrition and unhygienic living conditions (Raihan et al., 2014). Moreover, being migrants, these urban slum women need to adjust to the new socio-economic environment and thus they are overburdened with different responsibilities. Consequently, they are unlikely to seek medical assistance, in particular for issues related to their reproductive health (Khan and Kraemer, 2008). In addition, Alston (2015, pp. 153–156) identifies other gendered consequences of climate change impacts such as child marriage, gender-based violence, the difficulties girls face in remaining at school, an increased workload and the extra burden of repaying NGO loans.

These scenarios demonstrate how social and cultural factors influence the gen-dered experiences of climate change. In Bangladesh, gender power relations shape women's duties and responsibilities, and their access to, and control over, assets and property. Moreover, women's mobility and potentiality are also restricted due to several socio-cultural factors which impact adversely on every sphere of women's lives and livelihood. All these influencing factors shape women's vulnerabilities and their survival strategies, including how women relate to the country's climate change adaptation processes.

CHAPTER 4

Women's Responses to Climate Change at the Household Level

Women are primary users of natural resources, and they depend on local flora and fauna for their daily survival and family maintenance (Jahan, 2008). Ecofeminists argue that women's lives are directly attached to the local ecosystems (Merchant, 1992; Shiva, 1989). Consequently, there is interconnectivity between women and environmental degradation (Mies and Shiva, 2014; Shiva, 1993). In contrast, environmental feminists and feminist political ecologists argue that environmental problems that cause women's vulnerability are the structural result of a gender division of labor and gender power relations (Agarwal, 1998; Elmhirst, 2011; Resurrección, 2013). Nasrin (2012, p. 150) also points out that Bangladeshi rural women are more vulnerable to environmental degradation due to climate change but at the same time they have different capabilities due to their dependency on natural resources for food, fuel, fodder, water, medicine, and earnings for their livelihood. Similarly, Dankelman (2008) argues that women's primary responsibility for resource management allows them to develop different capabilities.

Using elements of the thesis's theoretical framework, this chapter intends to expose and explore the Bangladeshi women's contributions to climate change adaptation from their daily life experiences. Women's involvement in formal programs or projects demonstrates only a small segment of their efforts and contributions in response to climate change. They are involved in many more activities in their daily lives, particularly at the household level, which are very important to understand the gender-differentiated coping strategies and women's role in informal adaptation practices.

Household-Level Coping: An Extension of the Gender Division of Labor

Gender norms shape gender roles, which reinforce the "maintenance and tenacity of a hierarchal social order" (Singh, 2006, cited in Kevany and Huisingh, 2013, p. 54) and "androcentric and male biases continue to remain intact" (Panda, 2007, p. 323, cited in Kevany and Huisingh, 2013, p. 54). Due to a strong gender division of labor, the women of Bangladesh are more confined to households than men. Therefore, their activities are mostly related to family well-being, which plays an important task for their household's resiliency.

Food, Firewood, and Water Management

All types of reproductive activities are considered as the domain of women due to a distinct gender division of labor. Thus, women become solely responsible for household chores such as firewood collection, food preparation, and supplying household water consumption. Kevany and Huisingh (2013) argue that work burdens, particularly in agriculture-based societies, are distributed unequally to women and men irrespective of the region. Firewood collection is important because it is the main domestic source of energy: this is another major responsibility of rural women in many developing countries. Agarwal (2001a) states that firewood is usually never bought in rural areas and it is women who need to arrange its provision.

A woman aged 45 with five children from Mongla upazila, shares her alternative arrangements to ensure food supply for her family members, especially for her children. This is an example of how gender roles shape women's responsibilities:

> If my children starve, I cannot accept that as a mother. Therefore, I need to arrange food by any means necessary. When I cannot buy from the market, I need to collect food substances such as leaves, plants, and vegetable roots from nearby forests, and catch small fishes from the canals or rivers. Additionally, I have to collect firewood from bushes and trees for cooking to ensure the food supply for my family members. (IDI.3, 2013)

In addition, women lead in small-scale activities such as homestead gardening, plantation, and livestock (chickens, ducks, and goats) rearing have a significant impact on the household's food security as well as displaying resiliency. Hence, Glazebrook (2011) describes them as "resilient and expert actors" of climate change adaptation. Undoubtedly, Bangladeshi women are a major part of the contribution to global food security. Similarly, Kiptot et al. (2014) show that the involvement of women in agricultural forestry makes a substantial contribution to food security and to the economy of the household. This view resonates with the study's female participants from Mongla:

> We do homestead gardening, vegetable growing, and small-scale crab and fish farming along with our household activities. Although we do not grow those items to sell them, they fulfill the major share of our daily food consumption, which is a big support for our family. However, after fulfilling our needs, we do sell surplus items to neighbors or at the nearby market, which adds to the household income. (FGD.WG.1, 2014)

Scarcity of water resources is another wide-ranging effect of climate change, which was prominent in each of my study areas. As women are responsible for ensuring household water consumption, they have to spend a significant portion of their time and labor collecting water. In many areas, where drinkable water is unavailable, they have to travel far, but they do it as a part of their daily life activities to cope with the adverse situation. The United Nations Population Fund (United Nations Population Fund [UNFPA], 2002) estimated that girls and women in developing countries walk 6 km on an average per day to fetch water. The following statement from an FGD in a drought-prone area provides an insight into how gender roles define women's choices and force them to create different arrangements to cope. Women from drought-prone areas share a similar type of situation:

> Water scarcity is one of the main problems which we have been facing during summer and winter for many years. We need to maintain our household activities with limited water. Sometimes we need to drink less water to keep it for our children's and husband's needs. We cannot allow them to suffer. We collect the water from available sources whether it is near or far and manage cooking, cleaning, washing, and drinking water in different ways. Household water requirement is totally our problem, and we need to resolve it. (FGD.WG3, 2013)

Water management is one example of women's knowledge of the situation at the household level. Women need to decide where to collect water, how to carry it, and where to store and keep it safe. They also need to manage diversified water uses and purposes with the limited water quantity. Storage of rainwater during the rainy season for their household use has long been a common practice by women. Women use large locally available clay pots to preserve rainwater and maintain storage for use in emergency periods. A local woman from the Chila union (LII.4) explains that she stores rainwater during the rainy season, and she needs to travel 5 km to the north to collect drinking water during the dry season. Recently to mitigate the potable water crisis in this area, a local NGO, Rupantar, took the initiative of building water tanks to harvest rainwater; 10 water tanks were built in the area to attend to household needs in the community. This is a useful example of transferring women's indigenous practices to a practical problem-solving initiative.

In the Sapahar upazila of Naogaon district, a locally made innovative toilet has been introduced with the support of BDO (Barendra Development Organization), a local NGO. These toilets were made using local technology in order to improve sanitation systems and to reduce water use at the household level. Generally, women maintain these toilets; they informed me during the FGD that water use has decreased and that their labor and time have been substantially reduced as they now need to fetch less water. This practice correlates with Kuruppu's (2009) findings that diversified use of domestic water resources is significantly important for sustainable water management in the context of water scarcity.

In addition, some deep wells were built to ensure drinking water with the support of the same NGO in this area. Local women are given the responsibility of maintaining and managing those water bodies. Their role in maintaining community water resources is also satisfactory. According to them, so far there has been no problem in using the water bodies, due to an efficient management system which allocates specific maintenance duties for each area. To protect their own interests and benefits the women maintain and follow certain rules, which averts possible conflict among them. Faeth and Weinthal (2012) state that appropriate investments in water use, sanitation and conservation are essential in order to reduce vulnerability among the poor, promote security and ensure sustainable development particularly in a period of climate change.

Floating Garden—A Traditional Practice to Cope with Flood

As noted previously, Bangladesh is known as one of the most flood-prone countries in the world (Mirza, 2002; WB, 2010; UNDP, 2007). According to the Comprehensive Disaster Management Program Flood Map (CDMP, 2014c), 17 districts in Bangladesh have a history of 10–20 years return period of annual floods. Gopalganj is one of these flood-prone districts and is located in the middle part of Bangladesh. Nizra Union is within the Gopalganj district and is a floodplain with marshy land where people practice a number of indigenous strategies to cope with regular flooding, among them the floating garden. The settlements are scattered and located on raised land to avoid seasonal flooding. Local people and personnel from the Agriculture Department have commented that, for almost half of the year, the village remains under water as the large floodplain continues to be the basin of a large catchment area across the upazila (FGD.MG4 and LII.6). Consequently, about 90 percent of the village area is not usable for normal vegetation except deep-water rice which can grow as fast as 25 cm a day to reach a length of up to 7 m or 23 ft. and survive in water as deep as 4 m or 13 ft.

As the Nizra village remains under water for an extended period of the year, it is difficult to grow any fruits or vegetables except on raised homesteads. The limited space for cultivation of daily essentials creates an adverse situation for villagers, especially during the rainy season. Traditionally, to cope with this situation, the villagers build an artificial cultivatable space popularly known as a floating garden ("gaito" locally). The floating garden is the outcome of long years of cultivation practice in the floodplain areas, particularly in the Barishal, Gopalganj, and Pirojpur districts (Irfanullah et al., 2011). The floating garden is prepared using the long plants of deep-water rice and water hyacinth. Preparation of the bed of the garden starts after the rice harvesting period. The size of the garden ranges from 200 to 800 sq. ft. depending upon individual requirements.

Once the monsoon starts and water increases, the garden starts to float and can be transported from one place to another. During this time, different types of vegetables such as pumpkin, eggplant, and bean are grown in the floating garden. Due to limited access to dry lands, the gardens are also used as the grazing space for ducks and chickens. Women from their respective households take care of the gardening to meet their food consumption needs. This has been traditional practice over the generations among the villagers, who mainly depend on agriculture and limited freshwater fish. According to one male villager aged 75, the use of the floating garden in the village dates back at least 100 years (LII.7). He also learnt from his grandfather about the traditional practice to compensate for the scarcity of vegetables in the rainy season.

In the floating garden practice, women play a key role in carrying out the overall activities related to the gardens. A local woman aged 60 years of Nizra union, who has many years' experiences in preparing and maintaining her family's floating garden, describes the types of women's engagement:

> Men prepare the bed of the gardens, and we need to wait until it is ready for plantation. We decide what plants and vegetables will grow depending on our preserved seeds. Since the gardens are nearby, we can easily take care of the plants, how they are growing, what is needed when, and gathering for household use or selling. We raise our poultry animals such as chickens and ducks on the vegetable beds because at that time no dry places are available for rearing them. (IDI.7, 2013)

She (IDI.7) informed that the idea of a dry place (vegetable bed) that can be easily used for poultry raising also comes from women's knowledge. Plants get natural fertilization from hyacinth and animal waste and animals easily collect their food from the water and hyacinth. This supports their households' nutritious requirements in terms of vegetables and protein intake.

Women's contributions to such micro-level activities help with the provision of household food consumption in crisis periods and are directly linked to household food security. Similar statements were provided from others (FGD.MG4 and LII.9), where they acknowledge women's roles as household food managers—a part of their gender identity. This practice helps to save family expenditure and provides family income by selling surplus production to overcome the financial crisis after disasters (IDI.7).

This type of traditional native practice is gradually disappearing, particularly in this area, as farmers prefer to produce hybrid rice because of its higher yield quality. As a result, the native rice variety, which is the main element of the floating garden, has almost ceased to exist (LI.8). Moreover, the new road facility in the village has connected the villagers to marketplaces during the rainy season which has reduced the dependency on the floating garden compared to what it was in the past.

Such developmental activities can bring different consequences for women and men, particularly in relation to gender-differentiated household responsibilities. For example, in this case, women will gradually lose control over the sources of household food substances and some earnings if this practice does not continue, although their responsibility as household food managers may remain unchanged. This, in turn, can cause household food insecurity, as the purchasing capacity of the male family members may not increase. Ultimately, women may need to arrange alternative ways of ensuring household food provision, which will create additional burdens on them. Similarly, Goh (2012) argues that when male farmers adopt hybrid seeds and fertilizers, and abandon native varieties, more vulnerabilities for female farmers are created as they lack the capacity to purchase these items.

Traditional practices like the floating garden show how women's traditional knowledge and control over subsistence agricultural resources reinforce household resiliency. This type of practice can be a useful tool to handle long-term waterlogging problems; the National Adaptation Programme of Action (NAPA, 2005) also includes it as one of the alternatives (Irfanullah et al., 2011) of climate change adaptation. Moreover, the concept of floating gardens has been successfully replicated at the macro-level in many places. For instance, recently the idea of a floating school was developed by a local organization in order to provide education in a flood-prone rural village in north-west Bangladesh, where children could not go to school during floods (Epstein, 2015). Such traditional practices that have proven successful could be replicated in the southern part of the country as an adaptation tool where a number of villages are regularly waterlogged. These types of initiatives are a good example of sustainable and locally generated adaptation programs, even if women's contributions are often overlooked.

Women's Knowledge and Indigenous Coping Practices

Indigenous knowledge is not taken into sufficient consideration in adaptation discourses despite the fact that responses can be more effective if they are linked to the people's diverse knowledge, cultural values, and traditional practices (Kuruppu, 2009; Leonard et al., 2013; Rodima-Taylor et al., 2012). Feminist environmentalism's viewpoint suggests that there is a persistent link between women and the environment, which develops gender-differentiated knowledge in women that enhances coping capacity (Elmhirst, 2011; Resurrección, 2013; Salehi et al., 2015). People who are living with climate change impacts have alternative knowledge about climate variability because of their daily life experiences, which reinforce and develop knowledge and local practices in using natural resources (Briggs, 2005; Leonard et al., 2013).

Bangladeshi women are also adopting various indigenous coping practices which include seed and dry food preservation techniques, mobile vegetable gardening, measuring flood water by putting bamboo sticks in nearby canals and burning chilli smoke to keep the household safe from snakes. Women in cyclone-prone areas shared with me some other household-level indigenous coping practices, which include making "mancha" or raised platforms for livestock (goats, chickens, and ducks), dry fish and dry food preservation by digging holes in the ground; and pumpkin preservation to maintain household food security after a cyclone. An interesting food grain-saving practice by women was found in the drought-prone study area. They call it "mutha sonchoy" or "one handful of savings," which means they keep one handful of rice from their daily cooking allocation. After one or two months, it has resulted in a reasonable quantity, and they store it for use during a crisis period as an alternative source of food security.

Women reducing their meal amount or changing their mealtime are also examples of coping practices at the personal level. Homestead gardening and cultivating vegetables is a common indigenous household practice conducted by rural women. They continue this practice even in flood- and salinity-prone areas adopting alternative methods such as using plastic or jute bags to grow vegetables in order to meet their daily household needs. Women's home-based agricultural activities and livestock farming is a significant part of household adaptation which they provide for households as part of their duties and responsibilities. Dankelman (2008) and Nasreen (2010) have similar findings that women make use of their acquaintances and experiences in numerous ways to adjust and cope with environmental problems, particularly at the household level. SHOUHARDO II (2011) articulates diverse indigenous practices of the disaster-affected population of Bangladesh and shows how they make use of it to cope with multifaceted disasters. Similar scenarios have occurred in rural South Africa and in the African Sahel during drought adaptation situations. Local knowledge can add significant value to the development of sustainable climate change mitigation and adaptation strategies that are planned in conjunction with local people and address local needs (Nyong et al., 2007; Roos et al., 2010).

Subsistence Agriculture and Micro-economy

Women's roles in subsistence agriculture have immense value in supporting household food security in the era of climate change (Eunice and Gry, 2011). When the main agricultural production started decreasing due to drought or salinity, women moved to alternative arrangements in order to ensure food security for their households. Crab farming in Mongla and Dacope upazila, and lamb/sheep rearing in Sapahar upazila are two good examples of women's dynamic roles moving beyond their customary gender role in this era of shifting from traditional agricultural production as a result of climate change effects. Recognizing women's capabilities, many NGOs provide technical assistance for women to carry out household-based adaptation practices such as homestead gardening, hydroponics farming, and poultry rearing (LII.3; LII.11). In every area of my study, it is apparent that women are undertaking diverse micro-level economic activities such as forming women's groups, achieving small-scale savings within the group, becoming members of local NGOs and continuing to generate home-based income which, in turn, works as a household coping mechanism. Making regular savings of small amounts can make a significant difference, as the efforts of women in this area have shown in times of emergency. A group of women from Khulna and Naogaon area contend that:

> You will hardly find any household where women are not involved in earning. Most of the women are members of different NGOs. They form women's groups, provide training in different income-generation activities. For example, these are women's assets and usually, the male family members do not pay attention to those small earnings. We provide our family with food intake and also earn money by selling surplus production. This helps our families a lot in dealing with a shortage of food, especially the protein intake for our children. The money we earn from selling produce, we keep as household savings. We also have monthly savings in our groups and take loans from the group's saving fund in time of need. (FGD.WG2 and FGD.WG4, 2014)

All women respondents claim that their savings and support from the microcredit group have helped their families to cope with and recover from a disaster or crisis. Impoverished rural women of Bangladesh are the main stakeholders of microcredit and microfinance in Bangladesh, and they are keeping the sectors vibrant as well as supporting their families as argued by some scholars (see Islam, 2015; Loro, 2013; Rahman and McAllister, 2011).

Urban women also play similar roles in supporting the household economy. During focus group discussion with a women's group named "Mohazer Para Mohila Somiti" (FGD.WG7, 2014) in Cox's Bazar, the participants said that most of their group members are involved in home-based income-generating activities to support their families. Seashells are the main source of income since they get them from the sea and need not spend money collecting them. They can run small craft-making businesses dependent on these natural resources without any capital. Their children collect seashells from the beach, and they make ornaments, home-decorating pieces and household materials. Several beach-side markets have flourished thanks to the resources of the Bay of Bengal where women are the main informal labor source. This is an example of how women use natural resources in many different ways and support the household economy. In addition, local-level informants told me that women are the main labor force of informal economic sectors such as dry fish and food preparation, cloth embroidery, and street food vending in this coastal town. Rahman and Islam (2013) claim that there is a trend showing a significant increase in women's labor participation in urban areas of Bangladesh. According to a study by Asian Development Bank (ADB) (2010) in Bangladesh, women are predominant in the informal employment sector which makes up 89 percent of the total women's labor force.

It is clearly stated that women's life experiences and household responsibilities instigate them to adopt and carry on indigenous and local coping practices. Additionally, their contributions to subsistence agriculture, water management and the micro-economy are important tools for developing household-level resiliency to adapt to climate change or environmental degradation. Thus, women offer immense efforts at the household level, and that, in turn, supports informal adaptation practices.

CHAPTER 5

Women's Responses to Community-Based Adaptation

Women's involvement in community-based adaptation practices offers a new dimension in traditional societies in terms of reshaping gender roles and changing gender norms. Women's participation in various community-level projects increases their mobility in public places and creates the opportunity to become equal development partners. The following discussion highlights some significant areas where women are contributing at the community level.

Disaster Risk Reduction and Disaster Management

There is a close relationship between climate change adaptation and disaster preparedness, where women play significant roles in making local women aware and in encouraging the use of traditional knowledge to cope with disasters United Nations International Strategy for Disaster Reduction [UNISDR], 2008). When social and economic activities are interrupted during disasters and the affected community becomes solely dependent on external support, women intuitively take up the responsibility in order to overcome the difficulties not only for their own families but also for the communities. Evidence shows that women are the first and foremost respondents after any disaster (Nasreen, 2010, 2012). Women's roles and contributions are a critical part of disaster management and disaster preparedness responses to climate change. Gendered tasks, such as taking care of children, elderly, or disabled persons, reinforce a sense of responsibility in women and make them more capable of undertaking such social obligations. Moreover, they need to keep the household's food supply going. A woman from Mongla upazila describes:

> During any cyclone warning, first, I need to consider the safety of my young kids and my aged father and mother-in-law. After a cyclone, I need to think about my family members' food arrangements because they cannot suffer from starvation. So, I always have an emergency food arrangement. (IDI.3, 2014)

The Consultative Group on International Agricultural Research (CGIAR) Research Program on Climate Change, Agriculture and Food Security (CCAFS, 2014) states that within communities' certain people and groups who have legitimacy, and the trust of others can be effective mediators for the dissemination of information. A female union parishad (UP) member who is a member of the Union Disaster Management Committee in Mongla upazila demonstrates this concept:

> Now we can transmit the cyclone warning to the women, whereas earlier they had only the option of getting information from the male members of the family. Sometimes it would be too late for them to prepare to move. We like to continue this activity in order to save people's lives, particularly the elderly, women and children. Earlier, most of the women did not want to move to cyclone shelters, when forced. Now they are aware of the after-disaster consequences, so they willingly move to cyclone shelters. They heed the early warning about imminent disaster and take it seriously. We do not deliver only warning information, we also give suggestions about how to keep household assets and livestock safe during disasters. (LII. 4, 2014)

It was observed that women work as an active force both during and in post-disaster situations. Their capacities and strength have been utilized in local disaster management committees and positive impacts have been noticed particularly at household level. Another important aspect of the community-based program is that the activities are operated by the local community which motivates members to keep the program alive for their own interests. Moreover, after a disaster, women play a vital practical role in rebuilding the family and community, something that the male participants of the Mongla study area acknowledge:

> Women of our families and our female community members carry out many important tasks during disasters—their daily life experiences and knowledge are useful during and after disasters. We must admit that women have different types of survival and coping skills in emergencies, including food preservation, assets and livestock protection. (FGD.MG1, 2013)

Rural women's daily life experiences are important to relate with disaster preparedness and management as disaster risk reduction is considered an integral part of climate change adaptation in Bangladesh (Islam and Sumon, 2013). Field observations and discussions with local women revealed the diverse roles they play in the community in response to disaster management alongside their involvement in formal adaptation practices.

Natural Resource Management

Women's attachment to the environment is very different from men's because of their different needs, roles, and responsibilities. Nasrin (2012) argues that it is a historical reality that men use natural resources as income or monetary sources, while women utilize them to meet their basic needs. Findings of the study also suggest that women are more efficient at natural resource management due to the particular gendered nature of their work. Elmhirst (2011) contends that there is a link between natural resource management and certain types of gendered norms and responsibilities. Women are considered as the primary users of natural resources and they collect their everyday essentials such as fruits, vegetables, medicinal herbs, wood for fuel, and fodder from the forests (Jahan, 2008); for that reason, they use and handle them more carefully. The women of Dacope upazila prove their positive connections with the local forest. The head of the local administration acknowledges the positive use of natural resources by women:

> Since this upazila is adjacent to the "Sundarbans", the largest mangrove of Bangladesh, most of the people rely on the forest for their livelihood. Men continue to destroy forests by cutting trees and stealing forest resources, whereas women only collect food ingredients, firewood, and fodder to meet their households' needs. There is no such incident where women are found to be endangering the forest. Without doing any harm, they collect many natural resources as a household need or as an additional income source by collecting, processing, storing, and selling them at the market. (LII.3, 2014)

Thus, women are often considered as the custodians and promoters of biodiversity and environmentally friendly management. This notion makes them the prime stakeholders in social or community forestry in Bangladesh. The project manager of the local partner of Action Aid, Bangladesh explains the women's role in community forestry from his experience. In 2011, his NGO supported the plantation of 200 mango trees on two sides of the village road as a community asset and women were given the responsibility of nurturing and taking care of these trees. He recounts why:

> We find women are more responsible in carrying out their duties especially in taking care of trees and plants. From their careful nurture, the trees are growing well and they are expecting production within the next three years. This community forestry is their asset and they know that after four or five years these trees will produce a high yield of fruit. That will bring money along with fulfilling their consumption needs. This has been possible because the women's groups have taken on such long-term responsibilities. There are some such projects run by women and supported by local government and NGOs in this area. (LI.11, 2014)

Several NGOs have demonstrated the potential for "social forestry," whether in homesteads or alongside roads or railway lines, particularly involving women in Bangladesh. A study shows that women's participation in social forestry has increased from 18 to 29 percent during 2009–2012 and they are more capable in maintaining and making decisions in the social forestry program (M. Rahman, 2012). According to Sovacool et al. (2012) a major part of community-based adaptation interventions in Bangladesh is social forestry to protect ecosystems and diversify community livelihood to enhance their resilience. Women are the main stakeholders of this social forestation. The Community Based Adaptation to Climate Change through Coastal Afforestation Project was implemented by the Ministry of Environment, Forest and Climate Change, and 42 percent of its stakeholders are women (UNDP, 2010).

Women have profound knowledge about the plantation and ecological processes around them, since they are traditionally involved in homestead forestry as part of their livelihood. Women's involvement in pre- and post-harvest activities such as weeding, pest management, seed selection, and treatment and storage of harvest crops are important and integral parts of agriculture (Vyasulu, 2001). All of these agriculture-related activities are traditionally handled by women. For example, the women of Babupura union have used their knowledge regarding a recent pest attack in the paddy fields in an indigenous way:

> This pest attack happens due to the dampness caused by trapped water during heavy rainfall. The pest attack starts from the root of rice plants and spreads to

inside the rice and ultimately destroys the crops. The local Agriculture Department gives us pesticides but that cannot control the pests fully. After using the pesticide, 15–20 days later, the pests come back. Now we are using alternative home-made ways such as an extract of "neem leaves", "nishinda leaves", "bishkata juice" to control the pests. This preparation requires time and hard work in order to collect the ingredients and make it at home. We do it alongside our other responsibilities. (FGD.WG3, 2013)

Thus, women transfer different types of environments or agriculture-related knowledge and information from one generation to the next, which is considered an alternative way of solving problems. Natural compost preparation is another important function of the agricultural sector, which is performed mostly by women at the household level. They prepare it from the cooking waste, leaves, cow-dung and animal waste as part of their household duties and save money as the family does not then need to purchase chemical fertilizers. It is a nature-friendly practice and the best way to use natural household wastage. All these practices help to transform their knowledge and wisdom related to diverse environmental issues in rural areas from generation to generation.

The main difference between the urban and rural women of Bangladesh is the way they are attached to nature and natural resources. Rural women are more inclined to understand the natural environment, thus they use diverse natural resources for household food consumption and sources of income, in the process also creating alternative options to reduce vulnerability. In contrast, urban women do not have the opportunity to utilize these resources and they need to adapt alternative options to cope with the situation.

Environmental Activism

The impact of shrimp farming in the south-east coastal region in Bangladesh has been endangering the local ecosystem as well as the people since the 1980s (Perucca, 2011). The experience of shrimp farming and its relationship to the livelihood of women in south-eastern Bangladesh clearly demonstrates that environmental degradation is a critical developmental problem, which has a disproportionately negative impact on the rural women of these areas (Kabir, 2012). However, the relationship between class and gender often creates an unequal distribution of resources which negatively impacts on women (Thomas-Slayter et al., 1996). As a rejoinder, many grassroots-level protests by women to save the environment and their livelihood are found in many rural areas across the world, particularly in South Asia (Agarwal, 2000, pp. 150–151). Women's activism against shrimp cultivation and environmental degradation first appeared 25 years ago in southern Bangladesh. In 1990 the killing of Karunamoyee Sarder, a landless woman, reflected women's active role in the movement against shrimp cultivation in this region (Raj and Gain, 1998). A narrative of the incident is cited in Nasrin (2012, p. 165):

> On the 7th November 1990 at about 10.00 a.m., five trawlers carrying cadres of the shrimp lord came to Horinkhola to cut the embankment in order to set up a shrimp farm. Hearing the news of such arrival, the members of the Bittyahin Shamabai Samity brought out a peaceful procession, chanting slogans in protest of the shrimp farm. The shrimp lord's men attacked the innocent people ruthlessly with guns, hand-made bombs and sharp instruments. Karunamoyee, who was leading the procession, died instantly. Part of her skull was severed from her body. Twenty more people were seriously injured. To the local people, Karunamoyee became a martyr and the 7th of November is observed every year in memory of Karunamoyee. (Ghafur, 1999)

Another woman, Zahida Bibi, a mother of five children from the Satkhira district in the same region, was killed during a protest to protect government-owned land ("khas" land) acquired for shrimp cultivation in 1998 (Kabir, 2012, p. 68). Both cases are examples of women's collective movements to protect the environment and establish their rights. They sacrificed their life to protect their home and livelihood as a part of their activism. The Chipko Movement by rural women in India and the Green Belt Movement by Kenyan rural women are always highly acknowledged in the ecofeminist discourse (Rocheleau et al., 1996). Kevany and Huisingh (2013, p. 69) refer to another collective action by women, which has been carried out by strong grassroots institutions in rural Gujarat, India. The campaign "Women, Water and Work" demonstrates the capacity of women's groups to work through social barriers and continue dialogue with the state organizations in establishing their rights. All these examples clearly justify the view of women as a collective agency that has become a vital force in responding to climate change, particularly in protecting the environment and the consumption of natural resources.

Evidence from this study area also supports the idea that women's initiatives can lead to a significant change in the overall standard of life and can create positive impacts on the environment. Their life experiences motivate them to set a good example for their community in Dacope upazila of the Khulna district. Shrimp cultivation caused excessive saline content in the water, affecting the ground soil, which had an impact on overall livelihood in this area. In addition, after Cyclones Sidr and Aila, this area became increasingly contaminated by more salinity. The villagers have now realized that shrimp cultivation exacerbates the overall salinity level and causes natural degradation of the land as they were gradually forced out of their traditional livelihood options such as agriculture, homestead gardening and livestock rearing.

Women's suffering has intensified due to this problem, because the main source of household food security and subsistence economy has been substantially affected. As a consequence, women's dependency on natural resources has led them to oppose shrimp cultivation in their locality. Over the last 2 or 3 years, many lands were exempted from shrimp cultivation. As a result, women have started to engage themselves again in different kinds of activities, which contribute to protecting and retrieving their traditional nature dependent livelihood. This also is a positive outcome for the environment. A representative of the local administration in an interview points out:

> Women of this area have again started to raise all types of livestock (cows, goats, sheep, chickens, and ducks) because these animals' fodder is automatically arranged from agricultural subsistence products. Their workload is reduced by making use of agricultural wastes as fuel. Several NGOs and government supported initiatives are providing support to women through capacity building and skill development training, microcredits, and technology transfer. These are creating new livelihood options as alternative adaptation strategies. (LII.5, 2014)

This instance proves that women's awareness and involvement in environmental problems can bring significant changes in their lives in terms of reducing their workload, increasing the opportunity to earn money and ensuring household food security.

Many rural women's groups have been empowered to show their political will as their male counterparts do. Increased group unity and awareness have also developed grassroots-level activism amongst women. In addition, their significant contributions in community disaster preparedness and disaster management have proven their necessity in all the different stages of any disaster. Yet, in many cases, they are still struggling to establish their rights through reshaping traditional gender roles and norms. Overall, women's response to environmental degradation and their activism is another important aspect to consider as one of the critical factors of climate change adaptation discourse in Bangladesh.

The presented information demonstrates that women's roles and responses to climate change are similarly important for community resiliency as household resiliency. Women's knowledge about the environment or nature can help them to take particular measures at the household level to the community level to cope with challenging situations. This reinforces the significance of women's participation not only at the micro level but also at the macro level of adaptation. Women are the primary respondents in any disaster, including cyclones, droughts, landslides, and flooding. Moreover, women's presence in the public sphere has many positive impacts on society and environmental issues, as these problems are intertwined with their daily life. Women could relate some of social problems like violence against women, child marriage, girls drop out from school are increasing as the consequence of environmental problems. These positive aspects need to be capitalized on within formal programs and policy processes to achieve a sustainable outcome.

CHAPTER 6

Stories of Climate Champions

Resiliency is one of the important determining factors of adapting capacity or ability to cope with adverse situations (Tompkins and Adger, 2004). Nasreen (2012) states that women practice diverse coping mechanisms as part of their resilience to disasters. This chapter presents women's experiences concerning resilience in their own voices, within four different contexts of climate change. Their stories demonstrate that Bangladesh has already been experiencing a deep cultural change, particularly in rural society, in terms of changing gender roles and relations through women's participation in economic and development activities. The stories of four women show how they have confronted traditional gender norms, values, and cultural practices to craft pathways toward a more participatory development process related to climate change adaptation.

The stories of four women demonstrate the challenges of getting women's voices heard and establishing their rights. Their struggles reinforce them as active agents of development within the complexity of different geo-socio-economic situations. The stories convey women's ability to respond to climate change and demonstrate how their resiliency has increased as they confront different climate change problems and tackle the prevailing constraints of gender inequality.

Story 1: Anjoli Sordar[1]

Age: 27 years

Educational qualification: Secondary school certificate

Marital status: Married

Occupation: Housewife and member of Cyclone Preparedness Program (CPP) team

Husband's occupation: Driver (motorbike)

[1.] The real names of women interviewees are not used; this is also mentioned in Chapter 3 (IDI refers to In-Depth Interviewee).

Anjoli is a young woman from Bajua union of Chalna upazila in Khulna district. She was married to Khokon Sardar in 2006 at 18 years of age. At that time, she was finishing her school certificate examination. It was an arranged marriage which is a quite common phenomenon in rural Bangladesh. However, she was fortunate because her husband and father-in-law allowed her to complete the examination. Her parents' house was not in the same district as her in-laws, and the two areas are not similar in terms of geographical conditions. After moving to this new area, she found that there was a crisis in the supply of fresh water, and she noticed that the water was too salty to use even for household work. Her new family members collected potable water, which was carried by boat. The source of fresh water was far from their house, and they needed to cross the Pashur River that surrounds their village. Another problem she faced in her household work was that firewood was not easily available and they needed to purchase it. In her parents' village, they could collect it from their own garden or farm. She had to adjust to these difficult conditions to perform her household responsibilities. In 2007, she was pregnant, and she had to stop her higher secondary studies, because the college was far away and her physical condition did not allow her to travel regularly by boat and bus. Moreover, her husband and family members did not support her studies after she became pregnant.

In September 2007, the devastating Cyclone Sidr along with a high surge struck in their area. The warning of the cyclone had been given two days before, but no one could predict that the magnitude of the cyclone could be so destructive. People had been instructed to move to cyclone shelters from their houses and bring their valuable belongings. Observing the situation, she became quite nervous and anxious for her physical condition, as she was eight months pregnant. She was feeling a lot of discomfort and did not want to move from home to an unknown and common sharing place. She was more concerned about her movement and body shape rather than her safety because pregnant women do not feel at ease in a public place. Initially she was unwilling to move into a shared place where both males and females needed to stay together during the night. Later on she was motivated and encouraged by the female volunteers of CPP to move there. Moreover, she was also concerned about their household belongings and livestock, which they needed to leave behind. However, there was no other alternative, so she moved to the cyclone shelter along with her family members.

On September 15, 2007, Cyclone Sidr hit the southern coastal belt of Bangladesh; it was one of the biggest cyclones in the history of independent Bangladesh. It caused thousands of human casualties, huge loss of assets and destroyed major parts of the Sundarbans (the biggest mangrove forest discussed in Chapter 3), which is adjacent to the area where Anjoli lived. After taking shelter in a cyclone shelter cum primary school, Anjoli did not feel uncomfortable because there were separate staying rooms and toilets for men and women, and she was not anxious because female CPP volunteers carefully looked after her. There were a few pregnant women including her and three lactating mothers who needed special facilities and support.

> I thought I needed to stay in the same room as the men and use one toilet with the men in the cyclone shelter, but there was a different toilet for women. It made me comfortable to stay there. CPP volunteers were concerned about us who were pregnant and sick. Their presence changed my mindset about shelter places. (IDI.1, 2013)

Anjoli's family brought dry food like puffed rice, molasses and water to meet their initial needs. Later on, the local administration provided dry food, water and oral saline for the cyclone shelter. That was the first time that she observed the activities of the CPP and the role of volunteers during a disaster period. Their activities attracted her, especially the activities of women who were providing first aid to injured persons, helping the elderly, pregnant women, and children. During that time, she decided that if the opportunity came along, she would be involved in the CPP activities.

> It was an encouraging experience for me to observe the activities of female volunteers. They were taking special care of sick and elderly persons. They were trying to arrange a separate space for lactating mothers and pregnant women so that they could stay there comfortably. Their activities also included making the place safe and secure for women and adolescent girls. (IDI.1, 2013)

Cyclone Sidr brought huge devastating consequences to Anjoli's family. After staying one night in the shelter, they returned to their home and found that the floor of their house was under water. The kitchen and the cattle shed were demolished, and all the livestock, seeds and food grains were destroyed. They began to face problems of drinking water management and firewood scarcity. Because of these difficult circumstances her husband decided to take a new job as a motorbike driver for the transportation of people to remote areas, which is a common occupation in recent years in these areas. Earlier he had worked cultivating shrimp in his own land with his father. Although Anjoli's father-in law continued farming, the earnings were not enough to meet their family's household expenses. They needed to borrow money to buy a motorcycle for her husband so that he could take on this alternative source of income.[2] She had to ask for money from her parents. Two months after the disaster, she gave birth to a boy. Unfortunately, at the age of 1.5 years, her son drowned in a nearby pond while he was playing with another child. After this unexpected incident, she was severely traumatized, and her life became meaningless to her without her child. At that time her husband informed her that the CPP team was recruiting new female volunteers in their union, and he encouraged her to join it. She decided to get involved in this community work to recover from the emotional shock and this really helped her. Anjoli started working with women on awareness raising about disasters, early warnings and providing first aid care. She received training that developed her confidence to carry out her responsibilities.

In 2014, Anjoli gave birth again, and she now has a 1-year-old daughter. Every member of her family thinks this baby has brought good luck to their family, because her husband's income increased after she was born, and they were able to repay the money they had borrowed. This notion is quite different from traditional gender norms and values where sons always get first preference in the family. Moreover, her family members, especially her mother-in-law, were supportive and sympathetic about her predicament. She says:

> My family supported me a lot during my awful days. I might never have come out of the traumatic situation I was in if they had not allowed me to join the CPP team. My mother-in-law gave me great support by taking all household responsibilities on her shoulders. They did not only think of me as their daughter-in-law but also as a human being who has the potential to do something for the community. (IDI.1, 2013)

Because of her family support Anjoli wants to complete her graduation by using the opportunity of long-distance learning. She wishes to continue her work with the CPP as long as possible. She feels women's involvement in the committee helps significantly to make more women aware of their role during disasters. Women keep the community and their family members safe during disaster

---

[2.] Motorbike is a new transportation mode to travel in remote places of this area where other transport facilities are not available.

periods and contribute in post-disaster recovery as house managers. Anjoli expressed her concern:

> More women should be involved in community activities as that positively helps to keep them safer in any disaster. Moreover, women's presence can encourage other women to move to shelter places. Through our life experiences we realized we need more cyclone shelters in our area with special facilities for pregnant women, lactating mothers and adolescent girls because they have some special requirements. (IDI.1, 2013)

Now Anjoli has become an example of what courageous women can do in their community. Overcoming all barriers, she became involved in community disaster preparedness and contributed to household and community resiliency. Her personal struggle has positioned her as a role model of the community and an inspiration for other women. Additionally, her story shows that cooperation and support by other household's members is a vital factor for women to confront the challenges of gender barriers.

Story 2: Amina Begum
Age: 40 years
Marital status: Married
Educational qualification: No formal education
Occupation: Housewife and member of a women's group registered with Department of Women Affairs (DWA)
Husband's occupation: Agricultural works

Amina is a struggling woman from Sutarkhali union of Dacope upazila in Khulna district. During her life she has faced many ups and downs. Twenty-three years ago, when Amina was only 17 years old, she married a farmer named Abul Miya. Her father was a farmer with a small piece of agricultural land. So, for their family maintenance her father needed to cultivate other people's land as a share crop farmer. They had a big family with 10 members. Amina's marriage was arranged by one of her relatives who lived in the same village as her husband. She was fortunate that her husband's family was more affluent than her parents' family and she started living with less hardship. Her parents' house was in a nearby district and geographically different from her husband's locality. In her husband's village, all cultivable land was used for shrimp cultivation, not for agricultural activities. First, in her new home, she confronted problems with water because it was not drinkable or usable for household tasks. She noticed that her mother-in-law and sister-in-law collected drinking water from a fresh-water pond in a village next to their own village. Another difficulty she found was that during cooking and food preparation, firewood or traditional fuel like agricultural wastes was not available. Furthermore, she found that her husband's family had no livestock like cows or goats because there was no place for them to graze. There was no grassland or agricultural land, so it was difficult to rear poultry or livestock. She explained:

> After coming to my husband's family, I started accompanying my mother-in-law to bring water from the next village. I learnt how to maintain all household work with limited water though it was difficult to take bath and wash clothes properly. During menstruation it was more difficult to clean the body properly. (IDI.2, 2014)

Amina's husband had a large piece of land, which was leased to shrimp cultivators for a yearly contract. Her family members (her husband's mother, one brother and one sister) needed to survive on these yearly earnings. She started to adjust to the new environment gradually. She learnt new coping or adjusting strategies from her mother-in-law and other women of the villages such as preserving rainwater, small-scale homestead gardening and duck rearing, and crab farming to support the family's expenses.

After 2 years of marriage Amina became pregnant and did not have any knowledge about family planning or contraception at that time. She gave birth to a baby girl at her husband's house with assistance from a traditional village midwife. Due to her young age and weak physical condition, she suffered a great deal after giving birth. She could not take care of her baby properly due to her sickness. It took time for her to get physically well, and she needed to seek better treatment in a hospital in Khulna city after a local doctor referred her there. For that reason, her husband had to spend his savings, something that was not well accepted by other family members. From then she decided to start saving small amounts so that she could use this money when in need. She described:

> I felt very bad when I saw that my husband needed to spend his savings for me, and my mother-in-law did not accept it easily. That money was saved for my sister-in-law's marriage. I had to face psychological pressure as if it was my fault that I became sick. Women's health problems are not a matter of concern

> in most families, so my mother-in-law's reaction was quite normal. I was not
> in a position to challenge or change her mindset. At that time, I decided to earn
> and save money for myself. (IDI.2, 2014)

During this economically vulnerable time her sister-in-law's marriage was settled and her husband needed to sell their land to manage money for marriage purposes and the arrangement of the dowry. It was a big economic blow for their family. Her husband and brother-in-law only had knowledge and skills about agricultural work but in their area, they had no opportunity for this type of work. The male family members started catching baby shrimps from the nearby river Pashur but earnings were not enough to support their family. By this time Amina gave birth again to a baby boy and the household expenditure increased. Her brother-in-law decided to leave the village for Dhaka city to search for a new way to earn a living. He was the first person of their family who left the village as well as his traditional occupation. Later he became a construction worker and lived in a slum in Dhaka city. Amina gave birth to another child after two years and now has two daughters (17 and 13 years of age) and one son (11 years of age).

In September 2009, a big Cyclone Aila hit southwestern region/part of Bangladesh. The cyclone warning was given to the family by the local administration, to move from their house to cyclone shelters and take valuable belongings. Two years prior they had faced the devastation of Cyclone Sidr so they had experience in making preparations to move. But it was a very hard decision for them to leave their home. If they left, most of their household goods, cattle, poultry and food grains would be unattended, which might cause difficulties for their survival later on. Moreover, her mother-in-law was too old to move to the cyclone shelter. So she and her husband did not move to the cyclone shelter but sent their children with neighbors. They thought about their children's safety first, not about themselves. Although her elder daughter was an adolescent girl at that time, she was sent to the evacuation center to take care of her younger siblings. Amina was worried for her children, especially for her elder daughter because she was sent alone to an unknown public place. However, there was no other alternative to keep them safe so she had to allow her children to move with neighbors and requested that they would take care of her children. The women from a neighboring family kept her children with them and took care of them during their cyclone shelter stay. This is an example of women's strong bonding, receiving support and relying on each other in crisis periods. As she states:

> I always maintained very good relations with my neighbors and tried to always help them, so when it is needed we can rely on each other. We share our problems and try to support each other in any crisis. We have a very good social bond among the women of the neighborhood and for this reason the lady from the neighboring household took the responsibility of my children. (IDI.2, 2014)

Cyclone Aila destroyed the roof of their tin shed house. It demolished the mud made kitchen and ruined their livestock and food grain. Somehow their lives were saved without any major injuries. After staying one night at the cyclone shelter her children came back safely with the others. They then started facing a crisis of no food, no drinking water or firewood. To overcome the crisis, along with her husband and her daughter, Amina had to catch baby shrimps from the river and sell them to the shrimp farmers. She had never worked outside her home before and catching baby shrimps from the river was not a common livelihood option at her parents' village. After the environmental damage caused by Sidr and Aila their area had become more contaminated by saline water; moreover, for shrimp cultivation salty water needs to be stored inside the cultivation land and this impacts very negatively on the overall environment and human liveli-hood. As she mentions:

> Women realized first that this shrimp farming was affecting their locality negatively and that it had slowly destroyed their other living options such as agriculture, cattle rearing, poultry farming and vegetable cultivation. We suffered more because those were our main sources of household food security and income. Earnings from livestock and homestead vegetable gardens belonged to us. From these we could arrange food and firewood easily. (IDI.2, 2014)

So the women took the initiative to stand together with many victimized farmers to prevent shrimp farming in their area. The local administration, particularly the upazila nirbahi officer (head of the local administration), supported their demand to discharge saline water through the local government authority. They decided to make their area saline water free, particularly the paddy fields used for shrimp farming. From 2012, salinity-adapting rice has been cultivated in their locality and some seasonal crops have been produced. Women benefited in several ways from this change in the land use pattern. For example, they started raising livestock (goats, sheep, chickens, and ducks) and poultry because it is easy to arrange the fodder for the livestock from agricultural products so there is no need not to purchase it. They use agricultural waste as firewood so that the burden of firewood collection is reduced. They also started growing vegetables on a small scale adjacent to their house. She continues:

> I have started raising poultry and homestead gardening, which has helped my family to recover after the disaster and cope with the new environmental conditions. My support helps my family to overcome the food and the monetary crises. I feel women's involvement in these types of economic activities can support a family and make it more disaster resilient. Women can play a greater role through their economic activities and other daily practices. (IDI.2, 2014)

Amina thinks women are familiar with the environment of their surroundings because they depend on environmental resources to meet their family needs as part of their responsibility for their family. Therefore, agricultural-based livelihood adaptation programs are suitable for them. Women have realized that they can benefit from these programs even more than they had in the past. In 2006, they formed a women's group with the help of an NGO and in 2008 they registered it with the DWA. Their group's activities help the members to start earning a small income working at home by producing goods such as rice puffs, carpet and craft making with local materials and selling the products to the local market. She also thinks women need to unite and raise their voices about their problems. For example, now they are negotiating with local government bodies to solve the drinking water crisis with the support of the DWA and the above-mentioned NGO. Moreover, they placed their demand for more cyclone shelters in their area and good road communication so that the women, the elderly and children can move there without any difficulties during any disaster. Their group voices the need to resolve these issues with the local female UP members and disaster management committee.

Amina's experience is different from Anjoli's case, as she had to confront the traditional practices of gender power relations within her family. However, her struggle shows that despite challenges and gender barriers women cope with adverse situations, hence proving their resiliency. In addition, a women's group can create a strong platform for them to advocate their own issues within the community.

Story 3: Rafeza Khatun
  Age: 35 years
  Educational background: Higher secondary
  Marital status: Married
  Occupation: Community mobilizer, NGO

Rafeza Khatun is an example of a change maker on environmental issues in Sapahar upazila in the Naogaon district. She has been involved with communi-ty-related activities for more than eight years. She came to this village 12 years ago after getting married to Abdul Kader, a village farmer. At that time, she had completed higher secondary school while her husband gained his school certificate. She lost her father at a young age and was dependent on her brother. Her brother was not willing to spend money for her higher studies and wanted to shift the economic burden to a husband. She had no way of opposing her marriage and experienced very tough times after starting her married life. Her father-in-law and mother-in-law were not happy with her because her brother could not provide enough dowry money.[3] Her husband had no separate source of income; he worked as an agricultural laborer with his father. So Rafeza had to depend on her father-in-law and mother-in-law for their daily needs and performed all household work alone. She gave birth to a baby girl after 4 years of marriage and that was another source of psychological stress on her because girls are not welcomed in a society that favors male children, although she tried to face the situation with fortitude.

Rafeza's life had started changing after she became involved with a local NGO named Dabi in 2006. That organization started working in their village by form-ing a women's group. As she was the most educated woman among the group members, she was nominated as the team leader. The group activities included managing monthly savings, discussing their own problems, solving monetary or family problems of group members, initiating small-scale income generating activities and handling community issues. As a team leader she received train-ing from the NGO on leadership capacity building, group forming and saving to begin income generation activities; this training helped her to increase her capability and confidence. She had to train her group members and follow up with activities. Their group was the most active among the upazila and every member was engaged in micro-level economic activities.

[3.] This is a customary practice in Bangladesh that the bride brings money and household materials for husband's family.

After 3 years, that NGO moved from their village when the project finished. Rafeza tried to continue their group activities with fewer members, but it was difficult, as the majority of members withdrew their savings due to the termination of the NGO's activities. Then another NGO named Barendra Development Organization (BDO) started working in their area on climate change-related problems. This NGO is a local partner of Action Aid, Bangladesh who came to this region with a project on drought adaptation since this area is one of the most drought prone areas in Bangladesh. They started working by forming two groups in their village, a female group and a male group called "Gono-Gobeshona Dol." Rafeza was again selected as a team leader by the NGO of the female group. The group identified their problems related to drought and identified some alternative means of making a living. As a result, they ended up supporting their livelihood with activities such as lamb rearing, hybrid chicken farming and community forestry by the NGO. As a team leader, Rafeza had to monitor and follow up those initiatives to make them sustainable and successful. In addition, their group worked collectively to ensure services from the local government as well as other government services. She describes:

> As a team leader of Gono-Gobeshona Dol, first I understood the drought con-
> dition of our area as a problem of climate change and environment. We face all
> the difficulties as part of our daily life, but we never thought that women could
> identify their problems and solutions. We coped every day with this adverse
> situation in our own ways without having any formal knowledge. This NGO
> activity also helped to make us aware of local government services and how to
> use them to solve the problems. (IDI.4, 2013)

Such involvement with community activities has changed her life in a very positive way. When her family saw that her community engagement was bringing money and contributing to its well-being, they started honoring and valuing her work. Seeing her commitment and dedication, the NGO has appointed Rafeza as a community organizer. Now her bargaining power has increased both at household and community level; her husband carries out all household decisions after discussing them with her. In 2014, they built a new house for themselves, and her savings contributed a large portion. Earlier, they had lived in her father-in-law's house. Now she is empowered to make decisions about her own life. For example, she decided not to have any more children because she wants to give her daughter a higher education. She feels that they do not have the ability to bring up more than one child properly. She thinks women can be change makers for their family and society, if they can prove their ability through opportunities. She explains:

> Our involvement in formal drought adaptation activities has helped to value our work from the household level to the community level. Women's work has always been unrecognized and devalued in our society. So when women get involved in formal programs and monetary-related activities then family or society acknowledges their ability. (IDI.4, 2013)

At the same time women are struggling to establish their rights in every sphere to bring change to their lives. As a part of this struggle and along with her professional duties, Rafeza works with female UP members of her area to prevent early marriage for the girls of her community and to stop them from leaving school. As she says:

> Not only the girls but also their parents should understand that girls are not burdens. Girls should be given the opportunities for education so that they can be self-dependent. They should utilize the advantages and opportunities which the government is providing for them such as stipends, tuition fees and free education materials. If girls become educated, they will no longer be a burden for their family; I try to make their parents understand this. Social mobility is needed to ensure girls' safety and security while they frequent public places. (IDI.4, 2013)

Adolescent girls often face different forms of gender-based violence in public spaces, which restricts their mobility. Parents concerned for the safety and security of their daughters prefer to give them away in marriage. This is one of the major reasons for early marriage, which is a common practice in many rural societies in Bangladesh. Rafeza also encourages local women to involve themselves in community activities since as a group they are more empowered to utilize their agencies and social networks. She wishes to continue her job in this NGO as this gives her an opportunity to involve herself in the public sphere, which is still not easy for a rural married woman.

Rafeza's story shows that women's earnings and economic freedom help them to become empowered both at the family and community level. Their empowerment reinforces their ability to make decisions about their lives and their families' well-being; they are also able to raise their voice for women's problems and needs. This in turn supports them as they attempt to cope with any economic shock as a result of a disaster or climate change impact.

Story 4: Anowara Begum
Age: 19 years
Educational background: Secondary school certificate
Profession: Student and community worker, member of women's group
Marital status: Unmarried

Anowara is a young girl with the potential of future leadership in the Mohajer Para community in the Cox's Bazar municipality. Her parents migrated there 30 years ago from a nearby coastal island when it started going under sea level. This hilly slope was the cheapest place to pay rent or settle down at that time, as her father could not afford to buy a house. Her father had a shop near the beach area; she lost him when she was only 7 years old. Along with her two elder siblings (one brother and one sister) her mother experienced a lot of hardship. She needed to sell the shop after her husband's death. Neighbors and other community women supported her mother by taking care of them as she continued to do her work. Anowara's mother had many arduous jobs such as a construction worker, street vendor and house helper. After both of her siblings married, Anowara and her mother were still living in a rented house in this valley settlement.

Cox's Bazar, especially their housing area, is one of the most vulnerable areas for landslides and the inhabitants have had several experiences of confronting this hazard every year during the monsoon season. For this reason, Anowara was always concerned about how to protect and keep her community safe. She got the opportunity when the Asian Disaster Preparedness Centre (ADPC) introduced a program in 2012 and recruited her as a volunteer. She has been working as a volunteer for the last 3 years. After being selected as a community mobiliser she completed a week of hands-on training by the ADPC with the cooperation of the local municipality. With this training she learned how to rescue distressed people during disasters, what preparations were necessary in pre-disaster situations and also during the disaster and in post-disaster periods. Now she has established herself as an active volunteer with the objective of making her community disaster resilient. Anowara's work includes awareness building and disseminating early warnings to her community so that they can prepare and respond to any disaster on time. She is the only female volunteer with two other young male volunteers. Along with other volunteers she regularly visits different families who are living in areas of higher risk for landslides, keeps records of the daily rainfall during the rainy season and circulates warning messages to the community when they receive advance signals from the meteorological department. She describes her work:

> I joined the ADPC volunteer team after observing the suffering in our community, especially women, the elderly and children during every rainy season. Earlier landslides destroyed many families and took several lives in our area. Now we are more aware of how to respond before the hazards and what preparations are needed. My involvement in this project has made me valuable in my community. (IDI.10, 2014)

Anowara passed her secondary school certificate in 2013. She had a dream of higher studies but due to a financial crisis she could not be admitted to the college. Her family depends on her mother who is now working as a domestic helper for well-off families. Her brother started living separately after his marriage and did not support his family financially. Her mother's financial condition became worse when her elder sister along with her daughter came to stay with them after her brother-in-law's death. Anowara needed to start tailoring and stitching dresses at home to provide financial help for her family. She is also a member of a women's group at her community and was trained for tailoring. She received a sewing machine from a project that focused on women's livelihood from the municipality. Now her small earnings are supporting her mother by paying for household expenses.

Anowara's studies have been postponed due to her inability to pay for them, even though she has not given up hope. However, in the midst of her struggles, she is continuing her voluntary activity to save lives and to make her life meaningful. Although she did not express stress about her uncertain future, her nervous smile revealed her discomfort. Yet she hopes to continue her studies to graduation level and wants to become a leader of her community. She mentioned that some people with negative attitudes sometimes comment behind her back as she is an unmarried girl working alone with two boys. But she never pays attention, overlooks these sorts of comments, and continues her work. She is aware of the struggle of her single mother and female-headed households in society in general, but this only makes her stronger and more determined to face the tough situation.

> I have seen that these people did not come to help us when we used to starve. My mother had to work from dawn to night to feed us. Most of the people can show

sympathy but only a few offer real help. My life has taught me that I need to work hard to reach my goal and I feel that one day I will achieve it. (IDI.10, 2014)

Her family, especially her mother, fully supports her voluntary work that makes her more confident to step forward to future pathways. Involvement in community activities and her leadership role have helped to improve her confidence, a trait which many girls from the same society do not possess. This shows that if women or girls are guided correctly, given opportunities and supported with appropriate arrangements, there will be good leadership prospects for the future. Anowara could be a good example of a future change maker in Bangladesh if her ability is properly utilized. Climate change adaptation or disaster risk reduction is the new domain for women to prove their ability and develop leadership skills to tackle any environmental problem in future.

The chapter has focused on some significant changing areas of women's involvement and contributions at the household and community level through an analysis of their own views and perceptions. The four stories described in the chapter have revealed different vulnerabilities and coping strategies depending on socio-economic and geographic conditions. At the same time, their experiences have disclosed several aspects of gendered relations relevant to women's lives and environmental problems. Their stories illustrate that women do not belong to a homogeneous social group and thus they are diversely connected to their family, society, culture, and environment. Therefore, as their problems differ, their responses offer multi-dimensional prospects and insights. Women's individual-level struggles and efforts provide many inspiring strategies to address climate change adaptation. Women's increased participation in public spaces is a sign of the breaking down of socio-cultural norms and barriers, where they are perceived as subordinate to men (Sultan, 2010).

Many women have proven their capacity to become a catalyst for change, a role model for women in their communities and symbols of changing gender power relations. The women of this study believe that their involvement in the local environmental problems has helped them to access the formal rural power structure through community participation. Rural society is starting to accept women as the active participants of community development activities. Although the majority of women are still marginalized, it is also a fact that among them many have already created a new position for themselves in their own lives. They are therefore attempting to change deeply rooted gender norms through their endeavors in the social and environmental sectors. This is clearly an expression of their agency as they have managed to make their contribution in public. It is encouraging that many of them have a desire to continue their community work alongside their household responsibilities, which presents a positive trend of women's changing role in Bangladesh. This scenario also demonstrates that women's roles and relations within the family are changing in the era of climate change.

Resilient Households in Adaptative Societies

These stories show how women as individuals or as a group have expanded their efforts to develop family resiliency. Women's involvement in formal programs and projects creates a positive influence for other women in society. Women can identify gender-differentiated needs and requirements more accurately because women understand their own problems better than men. Gender consideration is a social and a political process, which is the core argument of both feminist political ecologists and feminist environmentalists.

Anjoli's suggest that women are no longer reluctant to move to cyclone or evacuation centers as they feel safe there. Their increased level of awareness can be mostly attributed to "pioneer" women's involvement in disaster preparedness committees and related programs or projects. According to Haque et al. (2012, p. 150) Bangladesh was able to reduce human casualties caused by severe cyclones over the years of the period 1970–2007 by 100 times. During the recent cyclone, Cyclone Komen, in the coastal region of Bangladesh on July 30, 2015, about 300,000 people moved from their houses to cyclone shelters and casualties were minimal (Chowdhury, 2015).[4] All new multi-purpose cyclone shelters have been built to address women's specific needs and old shelters have also tried to consider such needs when restructuring or renovating (Mahmood et al., 2014, p. 529). The willingness to use the shelters has increased due to the fundamental shift in women's mindset, itself the outcome of awareness raising, and motivational activities offered for the women, and by the women. Moreover, the overall condition of these places has improved in terms of gender sensitivity, becoming women friendly, due to the advocacy of women's groups and women's organizations.

[4.] This is according to reports published on July 30, 2015, in bdnews24.com. and on July 31, 2015, in the International Federation of Red Cross and Red Crescent Society.

The increased participation of women in disaster management or climate change adaptation activities has had a cumulative impact on communities in several ways. First, the traditional mindset of a patriarchal society is gradually changing due to women's increased visibility and involvement in the public sphere. Second, women's position in the household is being redefined through their economic contributions to the well-being of the household. Many families are now more willing to support and encourage them to work outside the home and rely on women's capabilities. Third, the findings also suggest that due to family support, women are now more responsible and confident to work for their community and their participation helps to implement gender-equal adaptation systems. The experiences of Anjoli and Anowara reflect such situations. On the contrary, Anima's and Rafeza's stories show how, despite the lack of support, women's participation in livelihood-based climate change adaptation programs increases their and their household's well-being and ability to cope with adverse situations. Additionally, their work has empowered them to confront gender discrimination and the obstacles that they faced as part of household gender power relations. Finally, the inclusion of women in formal disaster risk reduction programs has ensured more safety for their families. In turn this helps to enhance their resiliency, which is an important aspect of "cultural adaptation."[5]

Adger (2003, p. 390) argues that social capital develops through social interaction, collective activity, and networking between individuals or groups for their interests and well-being. Women's social bonding with each other develops into strong *social capital*[6] where other types of capital are lacking or absent. It also reveals that women's social bonding helps them to overcome the crisis that occurs during a disaster or climatic hazard as was noticed in the case of Amina. Women use their social networks to take immediate steps or respond to the household's food crisis, and to deal with financial needs for house rebuilding after a cyclone or flood or the loss of traditional ways of earning an income. It is a fact that due to the impact of climate change the number of female-headed households is increasing in both rural and urban areas (BBS, 2011). In Bangladesh. women's social capital operates as a strong support to their survival strategy, particularly for female-headed households (IDI2, IDI4, IDI5, IDI8). Silvey and Elmhirst

---

[5] O'Brien and Holland define the cultural adaptation as "one by which groups of people add new or improved methods of coping with the environment to their cultural repertoire" (1992, p. 37).

[6] Social capital is defined by Adger as "relations of trust, reciprocity, and exchange; the evolution of common rules; and the role of networks" (2006, p. 328). Shields et al. (1996) describe social capital as one kind of subsistence economic activity based on the exchange of small resources between neighboring households.

(2003, p. 873) argue that although women are often excluded from more powerful networks, a small network with their peer group builds social capital, which can be a potential tool for their empowerment.

The four stories reveal that when women's agency operates as a group they become more powerful in confronting any disaster or livelihood stress caused by climate change or natural hazards. Sudarshan and Bisht (2010) argue that many women's groups develop spontaneously as a response to local problems, which ultimately opens an avenue to raise women's concerns in the public sphere. Thus, women's groups can be an effective way to work within local government bodies for better and sustainable adaptation, something that Razefa's village research group was able to prove. Moreover, it was found that women's groups are more vocal about their problems and issues to ensure their rights and services from local government. Group unity resulted in achievements such as preventing shrimp cultivation, getting an equal share of community forestry and constructing women friendly cyclone shelters. They have shown the potentiality to secure government services from local-level government offices and their affiliation with the DWA has enhanced their bargaining power within institutional mechanisms. All these activities have a direct positive impact for the development of a climate resilient society. Feminist political ecologists have highlighted the importance of "gendered environmental politics and grassroots activism" (Rocheleau et al., 1996, pp. 14–15) in the collective struggle for equity and sustainable development, which is also confirmed by the study.

CHAPTER 7

Climate Change Adaptation in Bangladesh—Policy Frameworks Through Gender Lens

The history of climate change adaptation in Bangladesh is strongly connected with disaster management activities. In the last 30 years, nearly 200 climate-related disasters have occurred in the country, which have cost approximately US$16 billion (The Asia Foundation [AF], 2012, p. 14). After the independence of Bangladesh, the first disaster management activity—the Cyclone Preparedness Program—was established in 1972 in response to the 1970s devastating cyclone (Ministry of Disaster Management and Relief [MoDMR], 2015, p. 7). The Government of Bangladesh invested over US$10 billion over the past 40 years (mostly after its independence in 1971) to tackle the continuing disasters and to make the country disaster resilient (BCCSAP, 2009; Sovacool et al., 2012). Over the last 10 years the country has adopted a paradigm shift by moving from a response-based approach to a disaster preparedness and risk reduction approach (MoDMR, 2015, p. 10; Islam et al., 2011). The National Plan for Disaster Management (2010–2015) states that,

> Disaster risk reduction with climate change adaptation offers a win-win opportunity…Disaster Risk Reduction (DRR) is [the] development and application of policies and practices that minimizes risks to vulnerabilities and disasters, applies to managing and/or responding to current disaster risks. In this regard disaster risk reduction options are the front-line adaptation. Current risk reduction will lead to reduction of anticipatory risks of climate change in the form of adaptation. The disaster risk reduction options that best suit the user and [are] accepted by them will eventually emerge as adaptation options. (2010, p. 25)

Thus, Bangladesh has become one of the pioneer countries to establish an institutional mechanism for comprehensive disaster management with different stakeholders such as non-government and community-based organizations (NGOs/

CBOs) as well as other informal supports (Khan and Rahman, 2007). Due to its long experience in dealing and coping with natural disasters, Bangladesh has successfully developed institutional disaster management mechanisms at both local and national levels (BCCSAP, 2009). The Standing Order on Disasters (SoD, 2010) updated in April 2010 and the National Plan for Disaster Management (NPDM 2010–2015) are the most important policy documents in this regard (MoDMR, 2015). According to SoD (2010) each ministry, division/department and government agency should prepare their own disaster action plan and follow that during the warning stage, the disaster stage and the post-disaster stage according to their duties and responsibilities. The SoD was revised in line with the Hyogo Framework for Action (HFA 2005–2015), and the NPDM (2010–2015) was prepared followed by the HFA and SAARC Framework for Action (SFA). Both policies were developed by focusing on a more comprehensive approach to disaster risk reduction and resiliency (SoD, 2010, pp. 2–4).

Prior to that in 2003, the Comprehensive Disaster Management Programme (CDMP I), a collaborative donor initiative with the government of Bangladesh aimed to strengthen long-term disaster risk reduction and climate change adaptation through development policy planning (Luxbacher, 2011, p. 2). The CDMP I was the first initiative to shift from "a post-disaster relief and response strategy toward a comprehensive risk minimization culture that encourages disaster resilience initiatives" (Khan and Rahman, 2007, p. 366). This was the first long-term and comprehensive project of the Ministry of Food and Disaster Management that aimed to establish a mechanism of disaster preparedness and response at institutional and community levels through capacity building (MoDMR and UNDP, 2004). In the second phase CDMP–II (2010) aimed to "reach the most vulnerable section of the population and to integrate disaster risk reduction and climate change adaptation into community level interventions" (2010, p. 2). The CDMP II focused on community-based adaptation strategies such as awareness and response strategies among urban and rural populations, improved capacity of governmental agencies, and partnership and coordination at the ministerial level (MoDMR, 2015; MoFDM, 2010).

Islam and Sumon (2013) argue that climate change adaptation in Bangladesh has converged with two relevant issues, disaster risk reduction and social protection, and in local-level practices these are mutually inclusive. Social protection activities mostly include social *safety nets* to cope with natural disasters and other shocks; about 4–5 million people in Bangladesh receive some type of assistance from government supported safety net programs (Rahman et al., 2012,

p. 30). Ongoing adaptation projects are primarily focused on agriculture, water, forestry, fisheries, livestock, infrastructure, and health sectors, particularly in coastal river zones and in some urban areas (AKP, 2010, p. 11). These projects aim to strengthen the livelihood of poor, marginalized and vulnerable groups affected by climate change with the added elements of disaster risk reduction and adaptation to climate change. Coastal ecosystem-based adaptation is another approach that aims to build social and ecological resilience among vulnerable communities (Nandy et al., 2013). Therefore, in Bangladesh, the current climate change adaptation measures are mostly focused on disaster risk reduction and disaster resiliency.

Three climate change financing arrangements have been established to address priority adaptation concerns in the country: the Bangladesh Climate Change Trust Fund (BCTF), the Bangladesh Climate Change Resilience Fund (BCCRF) and the Pilot Program for Climate Resilience (PPCR). The first one is fully supported by the government's own resources, the second is a multi-donor financed funding mechanism and the third one is supported by the World Bank under the climate investment funds (AF, 2012). Therefore, many ongoing adaptation programs or projects are mostly implemented by the government or bilateral funding, or multilateral development partners, including the Asian Development Bank, the Canadian International Development Agency, the Department for International Development, the European Union, the Japan International Cooperation Agency, the United National Development Program, the Global Environment Facility and the World Bank (AF, 2012; Chowdhury, 2012). The World Bank, the Asian Development Bank, and a number of bilateral donors have funded a large-scale infrastructure project—particularly in the southern and coastal districts of Bangladesh in adapting to increased climatic variability and vulnerability. For example, currently the World Bank is supporting the "Emergency 2007 Cyclone Recovery and Reconstruction Project" with an oversight from the emergency of 2007 cyclone, Cyclone Sidr. The focus of this project is restoration and recovery from the damage to livelihood and infrastructure caused by Cyclone Sidr as well as building long-term disaster preparedness. The cost of the project is US$356.40 million and the implementation period is 9 years from 2008 to 2017. The project includes significant components focusing on disaster risk reduction such as the improvement and reconstruction of multi-purpose cyclone shelters and coastal embankments. Climate change adaptation activities include water supply and sanitation, and the agricultural sector recovery for livelihood and strengthening of local institutions toward improving the adaptive capacity of the target communities (WB, 2015). Recently, Bangladesh has been awarded the United Nations' highest environmental honor—*Champions of the Earth—2015*, in recognition of its initiatives to address climate change (United Nations Environmental Programme [UNEP], 2015).

In recent years there has also been a shift in approach from top-down initiatives to community-based approaches and coordination with civil society and NGOs (Shabib and Khan, 2014). In response, NGOs such as the Bangladesh Centre for Advanced Studies, the Centre for Global Change, Bangladesh Rural Advancement Committee, ActionAid, Practical Action, International Union for Conservation of Nature and Natural Resources, Oxfam, and CARE are involved in climate change adaptation activities in Bangladesh in cooperation with their local partner NGOs (AF, 2012, pp. 36–37; Rashid, 2009, p. 17). In addition, a number of NGO networks have been established such as the Network for Information, Response, and Preparedness Activities on Disaster; Campaign for Sustainable Livelihood (CRLS); National Alliance for Risk Reduction and Response Initiatives (NARRI) consortium; GenderCC; and the National Alliance for Risk Reduction and Response Initiative comprising eight international NGOs; these are the organizations that are currently implementing several projects funded by the European Commission and UK Aid Direct (Thomalla et al., 2005). However, there is still a lack of collaborative approaches on gender specific issues. Only GenderCC is a network that addresses gender issues in climate change, indicating that gender considerations are yet to be prioritized by the climate change adaptation sector in Bangladesh.

Existing Policies Related to Climate Change Adaptation in Bangladesh

Bangladesh formulated a National Adaptation Programme of Action (NAPA) in 2005, the first initiative of adaptation policies followed by the United Nations Framework Convention on Climate Change (UNFCCC) in response to the seventh COP7 (NAPA, 2005, p. xv). The plan identified the existing vulnerabilities and a comprehensive series of prioritized adaptation measures. This is the first national document where climate change was addressed as a separate concern. The UNFCCC created a special Least Developed Countries' Fund (LDCF) to support climate change adaptation and that fund financed the preparation and implementation of national adaptation programs in developing countries.

Consequently, Bangladesh developed its NAPAs and identified priority activities for both urgent and immediate needs in response to climate change (Konate and Sokona, 2003; NAPA, 2005). Led by the Ministry of Environment, Forest and Climate Change (MoEFCC), the NAPA was completed in 2005. Subsequently, after COP13 in 2007 and the Bali Action Plan, Bangladesh took the initiative in preparing a more vigorous adaptation plan in 2008 (BCCSAP, 2009). Thus, the Bangladesh Climate Change Strategy and Action Plan (BCCSAP) developed diverse sectoral plans, programs and activities and came into practice in 2009. The proposed activities of the BCCSAP have replaced NAPA's activities; it also identifies more detailed plans and programs covering a range of sectors. Moreover, it was decided by the government that BCCSAP would be considered a "living document," and that the document will be reviewed and revised through a periodical review on the basis of emerging situations (BCCSAP, 2009, p. xviii). There is thus room to add new priority actions while the present ones can be modified in future versions of this document if the need arises. However, Islam et al. (2011) note that as most of Bangladesh's sectoral development policies and plans were drafted before the BCCSAP was prepared, climate change has yet to be integrated formally into them. For example, the National Environmental Management Action Plan (NEMAP) and the National Water Policy (NWP) were prepared in 1995 and 2001 respectively. Therefore, these policies did not discuss climate change-related issues. As with the NEMAP and the NWP, the National Land Use Policy (NLUP) and the National Forest Policy (NFP) did not include climate change impacts on the concerned sectors (AKP, 2010). However, The Standing Order on Disasters (SoD, 2010) was updated in April 2010 and became the National Plan for Disaster Management (NPDM 2010–2015), where climate change impacts and risks associated with it were identified. Consequently, climate change and environmental issues were incorporated in the sixth five-year plan 2011–2015 and in the National Women Development Policy 2011.[1] Thus, the BCCSAP seeks to incorporate new plans and policies, or plans development in relevant sectors.

A brief information of two main climate change adaptation-related strategy documents, the BCCSAP and recently formulated National Adaptation Plan (2023–2050), are given here.

[1.] Chapter 8 in Part 1 and Section 36 in Part 2, respectively.

The Bangladesh Climate Change Strategy and Action Plan (BCCSAP 2009)

The BCCSAP 2009 is the first complete policy document for adaptation and mitigation measures in Bangladesh. Though women's issues were considered separately in the BCCSAP's six thematic pillars, overall gender equality issues have not been addressed properly (Neelormi and Ahmed, 2012). As a consequence, during the implementation of the BCCSAP at the practical-level gender concerns were not appropriately reflected. Since all climate change adaptation-related programs and activities are directed by this document, I have undertaken a detailed analysis of it. The following section analyses the BCCSAP from a gender perspective in order to reveal how it incorporates women's issues in climate change adaptation.

Under "Food security, social protection and health," the *first pillar* out of nine programs, only two have a direct activity plan relating to women. Those are livelihood protection in ecologically fragile areas and livelihood protection of vulnerable socio-economic groups including women. This thematic area portrays women as a part of the vulnerable group. However, the recognition of increasing female participation in agriculture, fishing and cattle farming, and their role in a subsistence economy and in food security has been totally ignored. As a result women's contributions and their specific needs are not taken into account when any livelihood-based adaptation activities are considered and implemented. Occasionally, when food production is affected by hazards such as floods and flash floods, droughts, salinity ingress, or saline water surges following a cyclone and waterlogging, food insecurity occurs (Ahmed, 2006). During any disaster women in Bangladesh suffer the most acute effects, due to food insecurity and malnutrition. In the case of food insecurity, women tend to take extraordinary measures such as eating less, resorting to poor quality food items or cheaper foods and not taking meals (Ahmed, 2010; Ahmed et al., 2012). This, in turn, adversely affects their nourishment and overall health. This is a common effect as is the long-term damage on poor subsistence agricultural households caused by climate variability and climate change-related hazards in Bangladesh. The BCCSAP completely overlooks these important facts. Therefore, no emphasis was given to the issues of food insecurity for women and other vulnerable groups regarding any disastrous event.

The *second thematic pillar*, "Comprehensive disaster management," covers the strategies to tackle climate-induced disasters through a comprehensive disaster management mechanism. Bangladesh is known globally for its disaster resiliency through its success in disaster preparedness and management. This theme focuses on the improvement of early warning dissemination to local communities (in cases of flood and cyclone) through awareness campaigns. However, no specific focus has been given to the problem of disseminating early warnings to the women in remote areas and there is no emphasis on involving them or using their potential in disseminating warnings. Practical experience reinforced by my findings suggests that women can be involved as potential partners in warning dissemination as well as overall disaster management if they are properly trained and well equipped. Lack of access to financial capital diminishes their ability to take hazard preparation measures, which reduces their adaptive capability (Neelormi and Ahmed, 2012). The current system of warning dissemination in public spaces often does not reach women in every household and they often do not get any preparation time to evacuate, even if such dissemination is provided from the institutional level in a timely fashion. The present reality suggests that a separate dissemination mechanism is required to reach women, particularly in remote areas. Awareness raising and public education aimed at climate resilience have been given emphasis in this pillar. However, no specific plan of action to enhance the capacity of women to better respond to disaster risk reduction is mentioned in the BCCSAP. The awareness raising programs among local communities about the impacts of climate change must include women-focused and gender-sensitive activities because women often do not obtain equal benefit from general programs. Their participation is shaped by cultural and religious factors, subject to convenience of time and place as well as access to opportunities.

Activities under the *third pillar*, "Infrastructure," focus on the maintenance of existing infrastructure such as road and river embankments and the urgent need for new infrastructure such as cyclone shelters, dams and urban drainage facilities. However, most old cyclone shelters are insensitive to women's specific needs, so women are reluctant to relocate to shelters, even after receiving early warnings (Ahmed et al., 2007). Such issues have resulted in a higher death rate along with injuries involving women in coastal areas in Bangladesh. Although the BCCSAP acknowledges the urgency of redesigning the cyclone shelters, it has neglected to include women-friendly design criteria. There was no directive to involve communities at risk in the process of building future structural measures. Therefore, most of the existing embankments and structural measures to safeguard people have been designed and implemented without any participatory process and without involving those segments of the community most at risk.

Under the *fourth pillar*, "Research and knowledge management," the BCCSAP acknowledges the urgency of carrying out research and collating knowledge to assess the impacts of climate change on different sectors of the economy for future investment planning. The state of knowledge is quite limited in particular areas, including gender differential vulnerability and capability to adapt to climate change, gender-differentiated behavior relating to carbon emissions, differential energy access, impacts on reproductive health, and mitigation aspects (KII.8). The main focus in adaptation strategies should be in supporting marginalized and disadvantaged groups, who are disproportionately affected by the effects of climate change. This has not been incorporated properly in the document, despite the fact that in this context local initiatives and women's knowledge base are critical to sustainable adaptation.

The *fifth pillar*, "Mitigation and low carbon development," aims to establish the low carbon development option because the country's economy is growing rapidly and the demand for energy is increasing. However, gender-differentiated energy consumption, access and carbon emissions have not been clearly reflected (Neelormi and Ahmed, 2012). The mitigation discussion is centered on the technological aspects of greenhouse gases. Men consume more energy than women and this difference was consistent across all income and age groups as men use more technology. Gender difference is linked most closely to energy use in the transport sector. This differentiated mitigation discussion is almost absent in the BCCSAP, although it has identified programs for the mitigation commitment of the government toward a low carbon development. However, as an energy deficit country, there is a need to recognize that the women in Bangladesh (especially the poor women in rural areas) lack basic energy services. They require facilities to access basic energy services, and the adoption of improved biomass stoves and other technologies (like solar home systems) as indicated in T5P4A4: "Study of the techno-economic, social and institutional constraints to adoption of improved biomass stoves and other technologies" (BCCSAP, 2009, p. 64).

Mitigation through afforestation and reforestation is another focused area in this pillar. It is expected that women will benefit from arrangements such as providing support to existing and new homestead and social forestry programs. The enhancement of the green economy is completely missing, while greater participation of women could potentially enhance it in the mitigation process. Women and communities have their own visions and knowledge on how to build and strengthen their resiliency to climate change.

The *sixth pillar* is "Capacity building and institutional strengthening" in climate change management where strengthening gender considerations has been identified as one program among six. Gender consideration in climate change involves the integration of women's issues in all adaptation and mitigation strategies and mainstreaming both in development planning. This thematic area opens a scope to improve the role of women in disaster management and involve them in natural resource management, especially in biodiversity and forestry. There is no clear position or clarification on Reducing Emissions from Deforestation and Forest Degradation (REDD), although gender consideration was mentioned here as a part of climate response activities. It is a courageous step that the BCCSAP took in giving a directive to "establish and build the capacity of climate change gender focal points in ministries and agencies to incorporate climate change considerations in all planning process" (2009, p. 72). The initiative is important regardless of any specific program, but no specific program or initiative has been taken so far in this regard. The MoWCA lacks both the budgetary and specialized human resources to manage the overall activities relating to gender and climate change (Ahmed, 2012). This is one of the big institutional gaps in the implementation of the BCCSAP's sixth theme.

Furthermore, the gender dimension of migration, which is directly related to women's vulnerability, is a glaring gap in the BCCSAP. Most poor households do not have sufficient capacity to cope with sudden and frequent disasters. As a result, they face difficulties in maintaining their livelihoods, which, in turn, triggers migration (particularly of males, see Chapter 3 (Falling into Poverty Trap). In the advent of this type of migration, the number of female-headed households increases (Guhathakurta, 2003; Neelormi et al., 2009). However, the BCCSAP did not give any special attention to this fact, so there is no program to support such female-headed households. In addition, under the flood adaptation program, non-structural flood-proofing measures were included, although the gender sensitivity element of these measures was not incorporated.

National Adaptation Plan 2023-2050 (NAP 2023-2050)

The Department of Environment formulated the National Adaptation Plan 2023–2050 (NAP 2023–2050) with financial support from the Green Climate Fund (GCF). This initiative aims to enable Bangladesh to pinpoint its unique adaptation requirements, formulate and implement strategies to address these needs, and make informed decisions on actions to safeguard vulnerable communities. The National Adaptation Plan (NAP) is an intricate process necessitating robust collaboration among government agencies, civil society, academics, and the inclusion of vulnerable communities. The NAP is expected to be the main strategic document under the UNFCCC process in the future to implement adaptation actions in developing countries.

The anticipated outcomes of the NAP are outlined as follows:

> **Outcome 1:** Strengthened institutional coordination and climate change (CC) information and knowledge management for medium- to long-term planning.
> **Outcome 2:** Adaptation options appraised and prioritized, and the National Adaptation Plan formulated.
> **Outcome 3:** Climate risk-informed decision-making tools developed and piloted by planning and budget departments at national and sectoral levels.
> **Outcome 4:** Nationally appropriate adaptation investments tracking mechanism set up and financial plan for mid- and long-term CCA implementation prepared. (NAP, 2022)

The NAP has identified 23 adaptation strategies and 113 interventions (including 90 high priority and 23 moderate priority) that encompass eight sectors and consider 11 climatic stress areas across the country. The eight distinct sectors are: 1) water resources; 2) disaster, social safety, and security; 3) agriculture; 4) fisheries, aquaculture, and livestock; 5) urban areas; 6) ecosystem, wetlands, and biodiversity; 7) policy and institutions; 8) capacity development, research, and innovation (CRI, 2023).

Gender Considerations in the Documents

The BCCSAP creates scope for taking positive initiatives in relation to climate change affected women. It acknowledges the urgency of carrying out research to develop a knowledge base in order to estimate the likely impacts of climate change on different sectors of the economy and to plan for future strategies. By utilizing such opportunities, a full understanding of the gendered impacts of climate change in different socio-economic sectors can be developed and that knowledge will help to design gender-sensitive adaptation plans. Although men and women live in the same geo-physical context, they experience differences in location-specific physical vulnerabilities as well as coping strategies in response to environmental problems. While the BCCSAP acknowledges gender differential vulnerability and capacity only to an extent, it remains a useful tool to develop a gender inclusive approach in climate response activities.

On the other hand, National Adaptation Plan for 2023-2050 has incorporated gender in a more comprehensive manner throughout the document. Health and gender are considered as a cross-cutting issue in the document which offers new avenues for gender-transformative adaptation processes in Bangladesh.

Gender Considerations at the Institutional Level

The gender-blind culture of any organization is one of the main barriers to a gender-sensitive implementation process of any plan or program in Bangladesh (Shabib and Khan, 2014). For instance, although gender issues have been included to some extent in the BCCSAP, there is often a lack of initiative among government officials to implement them, as in most cases they do not take gender issues seriously. Male-dominated institutional culture generally appears as a fundamental challenge for the incorporation of gender equality in the development sector in Bangladesh. Therefore, in most cases climate change is a gender-neutral phenomenon to them. A female environment and climate change activist working in a donor organization verbalized:

> The male-dominated government environment does not even see any connection between gender and climate change. They don't admit that it is a problem or that there is a need to develop strategies to address gender concerns. They usually ignore the issue, saying, "It is already covered" or make a joke by saying, "Why would gender be an issue when three women—prime minister, speaker, and opposition leader—are controlling the whole nation? Bangladeshi women are already empowered enough." This notion is common among many male government officials. (KII.9, 2013)

According to another Key Informant, NGOs have played a pioneering role in introducing gender sensitivity concerns in government sectors and have been trying to change the traditional gender-blind environment over the last few decades in Bangladesh. She continued:

As the concern related to climate change policy attests, gender advocates from non-governmental sectors and gender activists have worked to push gender as a key component or strategy that could bring some changes in the mindset of bureaucrats and in the organizational culture. (KII.13, 2014)

Although there are some institutional arrangements for climate change adaptation, the situation for gender consideration certainly has not been addressed properly in Bangladesh. In the BCCSAP, 11 ministries have been identified as line ministries to accelerate the climate change adaptation process. As the leader, the Ministry of Environment, Forest and Climate Change (MoEFCC) was given the responsibility to coordinate the process with other line ministries as well as having to keep track of developmental activities for successful implementation (BCCSAP, 2009, p. 20). The BCCSAP stated that:

The Government of Bangladesh recognizes that tackling climate change requires an integrated approach involving many different ministries and agencies, civil society and the business sector. (BCCSAP, 2009, p. 19)

Again the BCCSAP stated in its T6P4 (*Capacity Building and Institutional Strengthening*) that in "strengthening gender consideration in climate change" the MoWCA would be responsible and the key actor in coordinating and monitoring climate change and gender-related activities (2009, p. 74), as it is officially responsible for overseeing women's development activities. The responsibility also relates to the Ministry's "Women in Development (WID) Focal Point" arrangement, as its overall remit is to ensure gender sensitivity within the programs and policies undertaken by every ministry and agency. However, the ministry itself is not powerful enough and insufficiently empowered in terms of human and budgetary resources to perform the role effectively. Therefore, the MoWCA, even with the WID focal points arrangement, is often unable to mainstream or monitor gender equality progress due to lack of staff and technical capacity. According to KII1 (2013) and KII8 (2013), the level of preparedness for gender responsive climate change programs falls below the satisfactory standard. The Ministry has neither a strategy nor an action plan to address women's climate change-related issues nor is there any specific budget to do so. Therefore, the prospect of practical implementation is not very encouraging.

Another fact is that the government's officials have a low level of gender sensitivity, as most of the officials and staffs are male and consequently a male-dominated organizational culture prevails. Therefore, as an issue gender is always less prioritized so the WID mechanism is unlikely to become a powerful tool for the gender mainstreaming process in government sectors. Ahmed (2012, p. 19) argues that without a "strategy, action plan, and budget" it is not possible for the MoWCA to implement or monitor any gender responsive adaptation programs. Moreover, the MoWCA is not in a powerful enough position to put pressure on the focal points of climate change and gender in different ministries responsible for incorporating gender issues. A gender and climate change expert contends:

> Until now, main activities on climate change have lacked gender sensitivity. The position of the Ministry of Women and Children Affairs is relatively weak, and cannot enforce women's rights, which fall into the jurisdiction of other government departments. Gender issues were not taken up seriously in the Ministry of Environment and Forest, which is responsible for climate change-related issues. This is due to lack of awareness and specialized staff in the relevant ministries. Thus, women's issues are still less prioritized at the decision-making level in climate change adaptation-related activities. (KII.8, 2014)

Further, she added that some NGOs are trying to put a specific focus on training in gender-sensitive adaptation and low carbon development measures for representatives from government, NGOs, and academic institutions. The goal is to build the capacity of their respective governance mechanisms through training courses and workshops to enable future programs and projects to be more gender sensitive.

In addition, placing gender as a priority issue in the government sector is not an easy task for a country like Bangladesh which has always had to deal with many problems related to socio-economic development such as poverty, unemployment, and infrastructure development. Thus, gender issues receive less priority, and they are yet to be considered as a matter that cuts across climate change adaptation-related activities. In this context, an academic expert suggests:

> The MoWCA can provide policy guidelines, technical support and, above all, help to integrate "gender lenses" in all the activities undertaken by different ministries and agencies. In order to do that, commitment towards ensuring gender equality is needed first. If that can be ensured, this becomes an easy task to do by resource mobilization and hiring experts. So within government mechanisms

resources are not the main problem. The problem is the willingness and sensitivity to gender. (KII.7, 2013)

Focusing more on the scientific and technological aspects of climate change and attaching less concern to social aspects is another obstacle to incorporating gender issues in climate change adaptation (Alston, 2014). This kind of notion does not consider the human dimension of climate risks, differentiated vulnerabilities, men and women's distinct roles and responsibilities, and ability to cope with climate change, which is true in the case of Bangladesh. For example, adaptation to coastal flooding, waterlogging, and water-sheds ("haor") in Bangladesh cannot be addressed merely by initiating a few technical solutions such as building dams or maintaining submergible dykes. The employment opportunities for women and men, and their health and sanitary issues, need to be considered. The problem of differentiated access to resources and entitlements must be solved holistically. To solve the problem holistically, differentiated access to resources and entitlements must be addressed (KII14; CCGAP, 2013, para. 4). Therefore, the fundamental issue of including a gender perspective in climate change activities has not yet been properly addressed as a developmental issue, and institutional sensitivity still remains inadequate. This is the main challenge in terms of securing a sustainable outcome of many adaptation programs in Bangladesh.

To bridge the gap gender-sensitive training materials, capacity building and programs need to be designed and implemented through a proper gender-sensitive guideline.

A Positive Step: The Climate Change Gender Action Plan

Centre for Global Change (CGC), a prominent research organization in Bangladesh, organized a national dialogue on "Addressing Gender Concerns in Adaptation Discourse: Leadership Awaits Bangladesh," involving different stakeholders in Dhaka in April 2010 (KII.8, 2014). The workshop included a wide group of participants from the government, donors, NGOs, and civil society. Participants identified the particular needs of climate affected women for further action by policy makers. Such demands continued from pressure groups including women's organizations, gender and environment activists, researchers, NGOs, and government's development partners. They recommended a gender-sensitive action plan for climate change adaptation (KII7, 2013; KII8, 2013) to be implemented by the BCCSAP. As a result, the *Climate Change and Gender Action Plan* was developed in 2013 and considered a major achievement toward engendering the processes of the BCCSAP. In addition, to operationalize the mandate of the National Women Development Policy and the Sixth Five-Year Plan (2011–2015), the Climate Change and Gender Action Plan (CCGAP) can provide an effective mechanism within the framework of the BCCSAP.

The main objective of the CCGAP is to:

> mainstream gender equality concerns into climate change-related policies, strategies and interventions ensuring access to, participation in, contributions towards and benefits for the diverse group of stakeholders for the sustainable and equitable development of Bangladesh. (Climate Change and Gender Action Plan [ccGAP], 2013, p. 34)

The CCGAP integrates gender considerations into four pillars: Food security, social protection and health; Comprehensive disaster management; Infrastructure; and Mitigation and low carbon development. The remaining two pillars of the BCCSAP, "Research and knowledge management" and "Capacity building and institutional strengthening" are mainstreamed within the above-mentioned four pillars.

The ccGAP (2013) identifies relevant activities for these four pillars through an intensive gender perspective. Some important activities were outlined in the CCGAP under the four themes:

Food Security, Social Protection, and Health:

- Recognize women's contribution in agriculture to the GDP.
- Ensure women's access to land tenureship/leasing for cultivation. (2013, p. 41)

Comprehensive Disaster Management:

- Develop gender responsive policy based on disaster management, climate change and sustainable development.
- Develop adequate communication facilities to ensure the ability of women to reach safe places (cyclone shelters, flood shelters, killahs and others). (2013, pp. 54–55)

Infrastructure:

- Increase women's participation in climate change-related infrastructure development (planning, designing, construction and maintenance).
- Enhance technical capacity for gender responsive infrastructure development. (2013, pp. 65–66)

Mitigation and Low Carbon Development

- Improve women's knowledge on climate change mitigation issues.
- Develop women's entrepreneurship in relation to waste management.
- Mainstream gender considerations in coastal and social forestry programs or initiatives. (2013, pp. 79–80)

The most positive aspect of the CCGAP is that it has placed women as active partners of climate change adaptation rather than only as a vulnerable section of society. Moreover, the CCGAP addresses the unequal gender resource distributions, differentiated access to assets, information as well as power relations which cause gender specific vulnerabilities. Therefore, it has covered and included a wide range of gender-differentiated needs and requirements (both practical and strategic) in relevant sectors of adaptation. Thus, the CCGAP has created a strong foundation toward a gender-sensitive adaptation practice. However, the success of the plan fully relies on appropriate implementation and proper monitoring processes. This is the main obstacle for the success of many plans and programs in Bangladesh.

CHAPTER 8

Conclusions: Resilience and Adaptation—Fostering Gender Equality

Women's contributions to their families assist in the development of climate-resilient households and communities, which is important for climate change adaptation. Women's diverse coping strategies, which are mostly micro-level contributions, have a cumulative effect at the macro or the community level. Their efforts toward developing climate-resilient households and communities constitute a major part of their struggle for daily survival, even though they are continually confronted with gender discriminatory practices in every sphere of their lives. Further, women's experiences are an under-represented aspect of the climate change discourse in Bangladesh, because women's contributions continue to be dismissed and are not fully captured due to traditional gender perceptions.

Understanding Gender and Climate Change in Bangladesh

Bangladesh is considered the sixth most vulnerable country in the world to extreme events resulting from climate change. The country is facing climatic exposures such as sea level rises, saltwater intrusions in arable lands, as well as frequent hazards including storms, cyclones, floods, flash floods, and droughts. Factors including extreme weather with prolonged high temperatures are present and typically result in drought, uneven rainfall patterns, increased monsoon precipitation, higher trans-boundary water flows, and rising sea levels contributing to an increase in the extent of flooding. These climatic events convincingly suggest the presence and impacts of climate change. In addition, the adverse effects of climate change in Bangladesh are expected to increase the severity of cyclones by 2050 along with storm surges. Due to uneven rainfall patterns, new events such as landslides are taking place and affecting hilly parts of the country's south-east, thereby potentially creating further disasters.

As a heavily climate-dependent country, long-term changes in temperatures and precipitation have a significant impact on agricultural production. Increased temperature and lower solar radiation cause sterility in rice production and reduce the production of other crops. All these have a negative impact on peoples' livelihood, food security, freshwater availability, and overall well-being. Furthermore, the observed trend of rising sea levels threatens the coastal belt and may cause the displacement of approximately 20 million people by the year 2050 if the projected sea-level rise eventuates (BCCSAP, 2009, p. 16). Already as a consequence, a large number of people have been displaced by climate change and have been forced to move to urban areas. Large portions of this population are the urban poor, who are already living in poverty. The impact of climate change is diverse within every section of the communities, and it varies depending on class, geographical location, livelihood, and ethnic and gender identity. In this sense, poor women are more vulnerable due to the feminization of poverty (Neelormi, 2010). Moreover, in a country like Bangladesh, which draws on traditional gender constructs, daily lives are determined by socio-economic conditions.

Depending on the philosophical stance, explanations of contributing factors to gender-differentiated vulnerabilities relating to environmental change differ (Agarwal, 1998; Rocheleau et al. 1996; Shiva, 1989). However, feminist environmental theories overall argue that with their life experience and livelihood closely connected to the environment, women are more exposed to the adverse impacts of climate change and therefore they remain particularly vulnerable. Some examples from Bangladesh include walking longer distances to access clean drinking water in areas affected by drought and salinity intrusion, due to the changes in rainfall and sea-level rise (Alston, 2015; Neelormi et al., 2009); seasonal food insecurity from crop failure (Nasreen, 2008a; Azad et al., 2013); and male migration (Kartiki, 2011). Each of these consequences of climate change impacts women and men differently. These examples also have a poverty dimension (for instance, women who are from economically well-off families do not need to walk far to collect water. They have either their own water system or the ability to procure water). The study clearly demonstrates that in Bangladesh, gender and poverty are deeply interconnected factors that influence both women's vulnerability and resilience.

Women: Active Agents of Household and Community Resilience

Women's collective agency is important for dealing with environmental problems and women demonstrate significant interest in being involved in formal adaptation practices, despite the socio-cultural challenges that they face. Women play a vital role as active agents of change in community risk reduction, and they are successfully able to motivate other women to move to safer places during an emergency situation and to save their lives. Thus, women's visibility and involvement have become a crucial part of a community's disaster management and preparedness. Indeed, their role as members of disaster preparedness and disaster risk reduction committees has built awareness among their communities. This particular role is particularly significant across the coastal belt where the frequency of cyclones is increasing due to climate change, and this was found in the case of the Cyclone Preparedness Program. In addition, young women's involvement in community disaster resiliency programs is another positive aspect of climate change adaptation, particularly with the emergence of new climatic hazards like landslides in urban areas. Female volunteers have developed emotional and cultural resiliency among women and children who are the most vulnerable groups when landslides occur. Due to the intervention of the Early Warning System on Landslide Project, improved levels of disaster resiliency and quick response capacity have been developed among the women within the urban settlement of the coastal city of Cox's Bazar.

Women's involvement in livelihood development activities, potable water management, and community forestry is an important undertaking in climate change adaptation in Bangladesh. These activities are carried out so that vulnerable communities can cope with the climate change situation, particularly in drought prone and salinity inundated areas. Women successfully manage and carry out these activities as a part of adopting a new way of life. This was revealed in the ActionAid's project for drought adaptation. Local and indigenous coping practices like floating vegetable gardens can be an effective adaptation tool and have been mostly maintained by rural women over the years as part of their household's inbuilt resilience. This can make a significant contribution to formal adaptation programs if it is replicated in similar and newly affected areas.

However, women are mostly offered supportive and activity specific roles rather than roles that would regard them as active partners in formal programs and projects. The type and level of women's participation is mostly influenced by several socio-cultural factors where gender norms and power relations interact. Moreover, women's level of participation differs between government and non-government projects depending on the way women are considered, included and involved at all stages. The gendered nature of economic and political power relations to the access, use and control of resources is one of the key issues highlighted by the ideas of feminist political ecology (Thomas-Slayter et al., 1996). Bangladesh has a gender-biased institutional culture, which is more prominent within government institutions and significantly influences women's access to and availability of support or services.

Nonetheless, the presence of women's agency, through their involvement in grassroots- and national-level women's organizations that provide a platform to collectivize and raise awareness of their struggles against the adverse impacts of climate change on their livelihood. In their studies of South Asian rural women and environmental problems, Agarwal (2001b), Kabir (2012), and Nasrin (2012) show similar results. Furthermore, Campbell (1996) and Wangari et al. (1996) demonstrate that there is a high degree of political will and activism among women in Brazil and Kenya respectively. This study also reveals that women's individual and collective agency operate as a crucial factor to take up such initiatives. This reinforces the insight from feminist political ecology that grassroots political activism can play an important role in empowering women.

The current population of Bangladesh is approximately 160 million. Women make up half of the population and contribute significantly to the country's economy. They contribute to their household livelihood activities in addition to community development work, especially in rural areas where livelihood and economic activities mainly depend on natural resources and agriculture. Rural women are often responsible for subsistence agricultural work, household food management and they bear the responsibility for ensuring household water consumption and fuel. In the urban context, women also involve themselves in different economic arenas and contribute to the household's resilience by involving themselves in the informal labor market. Overall, the role of women is significantly diverse, depending on the geographical and climate change contexts across the country, particularly at the household level. Regardless of their diverse ways of earning a living, women are all active in making their households resilient by ensuring food security and water management, supporting the micro-economy through involvement in subsistence agriculture, natural resource management and the informal labor market. Additionally, they are maintaining numerous indigenous and local practices based on their daily life experiences and gendered knowledge to cope with adverse situations.

Gender relations are always a vital factor in women's everyday lives, and that these relations influence their experiences and knowledge, and these relations are not as simple as what is portrayed in traditional notions of power dynamics within the family structure. Power relations do not only operate between female and male, or between wife and husband, but also among the female members of the families as intra-household power dynamics. These dynamics have substantial influence on women's mobility, endowments, and access to and control over resources. Therefore, it is critical to consider these intra-household gender power dynamics when involving women in formal adaptation programs.

Women's community-level involvement through formal climate change adaptation programs demonstrates their capacity, and they have become an integral part in disaster management and disaster risk reduction, which are important elements of climate change adaptation in Bangladesh. In addition, women's activism to protect the environment and establish their rights has a long history across the regions. In many cases, Bangladeshi women also show their awareness of environmental problems and play an active role in preventing further degradation. Drawing from the ideas of ecofeminism, Shiva (1989) suggests that women share a close relationship with the environment, and they play a role as its protectors as well as managers (Glazebrook, 2011; Milne, 2005; Shiva, 1989). Women play an active role in protecting further environmental degradation, which adversely impacts their livelihood, and their motivation serves as a catalyst for involvement in formal protest regardless of the risks involved, particularly at the community level.

Many women's groups at the grassroots level and women's organizations at the national level are also functioning as driving forces for solving environmental problems, demanding basic services to improve the quality of life and establish equal rights. Women's multi-dimensional involvement often starts in the informal sector (household) and moves to levels of formal adaptation (community). Their contributions as individuals or as a group reveal their significant presence in climate change adaptation practices, even though this contribution remains unrecognized in the overall climate change adaptation discourse in Bangladesh. Thus, it is important that women be considered as the important stakeholders and as an integral part of the climate change adaptation process in Bangladesh.

Empowering Women for Sustainable
Climate Adaptation

Women's contributions to disaster preparedness, disaster risk reduction, and climate change adaptation have important policy implications. However, gender consideration remains an unrepresented issue in policies dealing with climate change in Bangladesh. Major policy documents neglected to incorporate women's needs and priorities as active partners; rather, they frame women as vulnerable and passive groups within society. The policy documents overlook women's potential and their contributions in a broader sense. Moreover, societal norms and organizational culture are significant barriers for gender-sensitive policy or program implementation. Bangladesh's male dominated organizational culture is a fundamental challenge in the struggle for recognition that gender equality needs to be addressed at policy level. Hence, climate change is still considered a gender-neutral phenomenon.

While the Bangladesh Climate Change Strategy and Action Plan (BCCSAP) and National Adaptation Plan (NAP) have included gendered considerations to some extent, there is often a lack of initiative to integrate them in government institutions at the decision-making level. This is because in most cases they do not take gender issues seriously. A gender-blind institutional culture is generally a fundamental challenge to ensuring gender equality in the climate change sector. Consequently, administrative mechanisms for climate change adaptation are not well prepared or implemented. Hence, policy support is vital to ensure that women contribute fully to gender-responsive climate change adaptation. A lack of gender consideration creates gender-biased institutions and limits women's opportunities. Thus, the study clearly demonstrates that gender is a core issue, and its significance is paramount regardless of the local or national policy context.

A gender-responsive policy process can support women's effective participation and acknowledge their contributions, particularly in new development issues like climate change adaptation. The gendered impact of climate change is a recent issue in the climate change discourse in Bangladesh. However, Bangladeshi women's lives are never separated from the environment: women are always reliant on it and its natural resources. Thus, the inclusion of women's issues in climate change and adaptation-related policies and programs in Bangladesh is important. Evidence supports that women can contribute and that their effective participation is vital for the sustainability of both formal and informal adaptation practices. This reinforces the significance of women's participation not only at the micro level but also at the macro level which is another key argument of this book.

In conclusion, women's diverse roles have proved that they are active partners in the country's developmental activities. Hence traditional notions of women and gender power relations need to be transformed. Although many positive changes have taken place over the years, women continue to face the challenges of socio-cultural and institutional constraints, which hinder their capacity to get involved. Furthermore, their efforts to fully participate are constrained due to unequal power structures. Therefore, it is important to address the prevailing constraints for women's participation in climate change adaptation. Moreover, their contribution needs to be acknowledged through policy reform and the mainstreaming of women in the climate change and national development sector. Women's individual-level struggles and efforts are an inspiring aspect of the process of change. Women's contributions in making their household disaster resilient through diverse coping practices are an important part of adaptation. Although women as a collective agency have become more confident in responding to such problems, their personal attempts should not be overlooked or ignored. Many women have become role models for other women and an example to be followed by others in coping, surviving, and becoming climate resilient. Indeed, women's mobility in public spheres has increased significantly, which is very encouraging for the empowerment of rural women. This is a sign of the Bangladeshi society's gradual cultural shift toward adaptation and resilience.

Many grassroots-level women's groups have directly influenced women in responding to climate change as they are the main driving forces in the rural development sector in Bangladesh. In addition, local government, with the support of development partners, has provided enormous support for women's advancement, particularly by involving them in income-generating activities, increasing their mobility and raising awareness about rights. All these factors encourage women to be confident in raising their voices, finding solutions, and expressing their views on this new social and environmental crisis. In addition, due to the influence of international bodies and development partners, the government has started to take the initiative to support the notion of women's inclusion and involvement in climate change adaptation. The formulation of the CCGAP is a powerful platform and opportunity to implement gender-responsive adaptation processes.

Notwithstanding many positive and inspiring achievements, Bangladeshi women still need to confront several existing structural and socio-cultural constraints.

Persistent unequal gender power relations within the household, community or society undermine women's capability and restrict their engagement in certain types of activities that can prove them equal to men. This situation is reinforced by many unequal gender norms and practices, which are the main challenges for women in becoming more active partners in climate change adaptation. Due to this cultural mindset, women's contributions are mostly undermined and undervalued. As a result, they are deprived of institutional and governmental support, which places them in an even more vulnerable position. Indeed, women have been considered to be recipients of, not active partners in, formal climate change adaptation processes. These factors thus undermine women's struggles, ignore their voices, and do not fully acknowledge their contributions to family or society. This is part of their continual struggle for survival within broader environmental politics and activism.

Changing gender relations in every sphere of women's life and engendering an organization's culture and policy process can reduce this gap. Mainstreaming gender issues, particularly in national development policies, disaster preparedness, and national economic planning, can help to formulate a robust gender-responsive climate change adaptation policy. In addition, community based consultative processes that involve every section of the society, particularly those who are more vulnerable to climate change, can enhance the gender responsiveness of any adaptation policy. Hence, there is a need to revisit the prevailing understanding of women's roles and positions in climate change adaptation. This reevaluation should underscore how women actively contribute to building resilience at the household level and examine the cascading effects of this resilience on a broader scale. Recognizing women's overall resilience and understanding the dynamic nature of gender relations becomes imperative in the discourse surrounding climate change adaptation. Hence, implementing a gender transformative climate change adaptation process is essential to attain the Sustainable Development Goals in Bangladesh.

BIBLIOGRAPHY

ACR (Association for Climate Refugees). 2012. *Climate "Refugees" in Bangladesh—Answering the Basics: The Where, How, Who and How Many?* ACR.

ADB (Asian Development Bank). 2010. *The Informal Sector and Informal Employment in Bangladesh: Country Report–2010*. ADB.

ADB (Asian Development Bank). 2009. *The Economics of Climate Change in Southeast Asia: A Regional Review*. ADB.

Adger, N. 2003. "Social Capital, Collective Action, and Adaptation to Climate Change." *Economic Geography* 79 (4): 387–404.

Adger, N. 2006. "Vulnerability." *Global Environmental Change* 16 (3): 268–281. http://doi.org/10.1016/j.gloenvcha.2006.02.006.

Adger, N., S. Huq, K. Brown, D. Conway, and M. Hulme. 2003. "Adaptation to Climate Change in the Developing World." *Progress in Development Studies* 3 (3): 179–195.

Adger, W. N., J. M. Pulhin, J. Barnett, G. D. Dabelko, G. K. Hovelsrud, M. Levy, Ú. Oswald Spring, and C. H. Vogel. 2014. "Human Security." In *Climate Change 2014: Impacts, Adaptation, and Vulnerability—Part A: Global and Sectoral Aspects—Contribution of Working Group II to the Fifth Assessment Report of the Intergovernmental Panel on Climate Change*, edited by Christopher B. Field and Vicente R. Barros. Cambridge University Press.

ADPC (Asian Disaster Preparedness Centre). 2013. *Assessment Report of Community Based Early Warning System (CBEWS) on Landslide: Cox's Bazar and Teknaf Municipality*. ADPC.

ADPC (Asian Disaster Preparedness Centre). 2010. *Concept Note on Community Level Landslide Risk Management in Chittagong*. ADPC.

AF (The Asia Foundation). 2012. *A Situation Analysis of Climate Change Adaptation Initiatives in Bangladesh*. AF.

Afsar, R. 2003. "Internal Migration and the Development Nexus: The Case of Bangladesh." Paper presented at the Regional Conference on Migration, Development and Pro-Poor Policy Choices in Asia: Refugee and Migratory Movements Research Unit, Dhaka and UK Department for International Development, London, June 22–24, 2003.

Agarwal, B. 1994. *A Field of One's Own: Gender and Land Rights in South Asia.* Cambridge University Press.

Agarwal, B. 2010. "Does Women's Proportional Strength Affect Their Participation? Governing Local Forests in South Asia." *World Development* 38 (1): 98–112.

Agarwal, B. 2009. "Rule Making in Community Forestry Institutions: The Difference Women Make." *Ecological Economics* 68 (8): 2296–2308.

Agarwal, B. 2001a. "Participatory Exclusions, Community Forestry and Gender: An Analysis for South Asia and a Conceptual Framework." *World Development* 29 (10): 1623–1648.

Agarwal, B. 2001b. "A Challenge for Ecofeminism: Gender, Greening and Community Forestry in India." *Women and Environments International* 52–53: 12–15.

Agarwal, B. 2000. "Conceptualising Environmental Collective Action: Why Gender Matters?" *Cambridge Journal of Economics* 24 (3): 283–310.

Agarwal, B. 1998. "The Gender and Environment Debate." In *Political Ecology: Global and Political*, edited by R. Keil, et al. Routledge.

Agarwal, B. 1997a. " 'Bargaining' and Gender Relations: Within and Beyond the Household." *Feminist Economics* 3 (1): 1–51.

Agarwal, B. 1997b. "Re-Sounding the Alert- Gender, Resources and Community Action." *World Development* 25 (9): 1373–1380.

Agarwal, B. 1992. "The Gender and Environment Debate: Lessons from India." *Feminist Studies* 18 (1): 119–158.

Agrawala, S., T. Ota, A. U. Ahmed, J. Smith, and M. Van Aalst. 2003. *Development and Climate Change in Bangladesh Focus on Coastal Flooding and the Sundarbans*. Organisation for Economic Co-Operation and Development.

Ahammed, S. 2010. "Impact of Tourism in Cox's Bazar, Bangladesh." Masters' thesis, North South University.

Ahmed, A. U. 2010. *Climate Change and Food Security in Bangladesh*. Report Prepared for Oxfam Novib, Centre for Global Change (CGC).

Ahmed, A. U. 2006. *Bangladesh Climate Impacts and Vulnerability: A Synthesis*. Climate Change Cell, Department of Environment Comprehensive Disaster Management Programme, Government of the People's Republic of Bangladesh.

Ahmed, A. U., M. Alam, and A. Rahman. 1999. "Adaptation to Climate Change in Bangladesh: Future Outlook." In *Vulnerability and Adaptation to Climate Change for Bangladesh,* edited by S. Huq, et al. Springer.

Ahmed, A. U., S. R. Hassan, B. Etzold, and S. Neelormi. 2012. *Rainfall, Food Security and Human Mobility: Case Study Bangladesh*. Report #2, Where the Rain Falls Project, United Nations University, Institute for Environment and Human Security (UNU-EHS).

Ahmed, A. U., S. Neelormi, N. Adri, M. S. Alam, and K. Nuruzzaman. 2007. *Climate Change, Gender and Special Vulnerable Groups in Bangladesh*. Draft Final Report, BASTOB and Center for Global Change (CGC), Ministry of Environment and Forest, Government of the People's Republic of Bangladesh, August.

Ahmed, N. 2012. *Gender and Climate Change in Bangladesh: The Role of Institutions in Reducing Gender Gaps in Adaptation Program*. Social Development Papers, a s\Summary of ESW Report no. P125705, Paper no 126, The World Bank.

Ahmed, S., and P. Maitra. 2010. "Gender Wage Discrimination in Rural and Urban Labour Markets of Bangladesh." *Oxford Development Studies* 38 (1): 83–112.

Ahsan, R., S. Karuppannan, and J. Kellett. 2011. "Climate Migration and Urban Planning System: A Study of Bangladesh." *Environmental Justice* 4 (3): 163–170.

AKP (Adaptation Knowledge Platform). 2010. *Scoping Assessment on Climate Change Adaptation in Bangladesh*. Thailand Regional Climate Change Adaptation Knowledge Platform for Asia.

Alam, K. 2015. "Farmers' Adaptation to Water Scarcity in Drought-Prone Environments: A Case Study of Rajshahi District, Bangladesh." *Agricultural Water Management* 148: 196–206.

Alam, M., A. Nishat, and S. M. Siddiqui. 1998. "Water Resources Vulnerability to Climate Change with Special Reference to Inundation." In *Vulnerability and Adaptation to Climate Change for Bangladesh,* edited by S. Huq, Z. Karim, M. Asaduzzman, and F. Mahtab. Kluwer Academic Publishers.

Alston, M. 2015. *Women and Climate Change in Bangladesh.* Routledge.

Alston, M. 2014. "Gender Mainstreaming and Climate Change." *Women's Studies International Forum* 47: 287–294.

Arora-Jonsson, S. 2011. "Virtue and Vulnerability: Discourses on Women, Gender and Climate Change." *Global Environmental Change* 21 (2): 744–751.

Atiq, R., M. Alam, S. S. Alam, R. M. Uzzaman, R. Mariam, and R. Golam. 2007. *Background Paper on Risks, Vulnerability and Adaptation in Bangladesh.* UNDP Human Development Report–2007.

Ayers, J., and T. Forsyth. 2009. "Community-Based Adaptation to Climate Change." *Environment: Science and Policy for Sustainable Development* 51 (4): 22–31.

Ayers, J., and S. Huq. 2009. "The Value of Linking Mitigation and Adaptation: A Case Study of Bangladesh." *Environmental Management* 43 (5): 753–764.

Azad, K., M. Hossain, and M. Nasreen. 2013. "Flood-Induced Vulnerabilities and Problems Encountered by Women in Northern Bangladesh." *International Journal of Disaster Risk Science* 4 (4): 190–199.

Azad, J. and B. Pritchard. 2023. "The Importance of Women's Roles in Adaptive Capacity and Resilience to Flooding in Rural Bangladesh." *International Journal of Disaster Risk Reduction* 90: 103660, https://doi.org/10.1016/j.ijdrr.2023.103660. (https://www.sciencedirect.com/science/article/pii/S2212420923001401).

Azim, F. 2010. "The New 21st-Century Women." In *Mapping Women's Empowerment: Experiences from Bangladesh, India and Pakistan,* edited by F. Azim and M. Sultan. UPL & BDI.

Bachman, R., and R. K. Schutt. 2014. *The Practice of Research in Criminology and Criminal Justice.* 5th ed. Sage.

Banerjee, D., and M. Mayerfeld Bell. 2007. "Eco-Gender: Locating Gender in the Environmental Social Sciences." *Society and Natural Resources* 20 (1): 3–19.

Bangladesh Climate Change Country Study. 1997. *Assessment of Vulnerability and Adaptation to Climate Change* (Final Report). Department of Environment, Ministry of Environment, Forest and Climate Change, Government of Peoples Republic Bangladesh.

Bangladesh Sample Vital Statistics. 2022. Bangladesh Bureau of Statistics, Statistics and Information Division. Ministry of Planning. Government of Peoples Republic Bangladesh.

Basit, N. 2003. "Manual or Electronic? The Role of Coding in Qualitative Data Analysis." *Educational Research* 45 (2): 143–154.

BBS (Bangladesh Bureau of Statistics). 2022a. *Population and Housing Census.* Socio-Economic and Demographic Report. Statistics and Informatics Division (SID), Ministry of Planning, Government of Bangladesh (GoB).

BBS (Bangladesh Bureau of Statistics). 2022b. *Household Income and Expenditure Survey (HIES).* Statistics and Informatics Division (SID), Ministry of Planning, Government of Bangladesh (GoB).

BBS (Bangladesh Bureau of Statistics). 2022c. *Labour Force Survey (LFS).* Statistics and Informatics Division (SID), Ministry of Planning, Government of Bangladesh (GoB).

BBS (Bangladesh Bureau of Statistics). (2018). *Bangladesh Education Statistics (BES).* Statistics and Informatics Division (SID), Ministry of Planning, Government of Bangladesh (GoB).

BBS (Bangladesh Bureau of Statistics). 2011. *Population and Housing Census.* Socio-Economic and Demographic Report. Statistics and Informatics Division (SID), Ministry of Planning, Government of Bangladesh (GoB).

BCCSAP (Bangladesh Climate Change Strategy and Action Plan). 2009. *Ministry of Environment Forest and Climate Change*, Government of the People's Republic of Bangladesh.

Beddington, J. 2011. *Migration and Global Environmental Change: Future Challenges and Opportunities.* Foresight Report, The Government Office for Science, UK.

Begum, A. 2012. "Women's Participation in Union Parishads: A Quest from a Compassionate Legal Approach in Bangladesh from an International Perspective." *Journal of South Asia Studies* 35 (3): 570–595.

Begum, M. 2012. *Muktijudde Nari* [Women in Liberation War]. Prothoma Publisher.

Begum, S. 1997. *Health Dimension of Poverty in Rural Bangladesh: Some Evidence.* Bangladesh Institute of Development Studies (BIDS).

Briggs, J. 2005. "The Use of Indigenous Knowledge in Development: Problems and Challenges." *Progress in Development Studies* 5 (2): 99–114.

BSDO (Barenrda Social Development Organization). 2013. *Annual Report (January–December.* BSDO.

Buckingham, S. 2004. "Ecofeminism in the Twenty First Century." *Geographical Journal* 170 (2): 146–155.

Buckingham-Hatfield, S. 2000. *Gender and Environment.* Routledge.

Campbell, C. 1996. "Out on the Front Lines but Still Struggling for Voice: Women in the Rubber Tappers' Defense of the Forest in Xapuri, Acre, Brazil." In *Feminist Political Ecology: Global Issues and Local Experiences*, edited by D. Rocheleau, et al. Routledge.

Cannon, T. 2002. "Gender and Climate Hazards in Bangladesh." *Gender and Development* 10 (2): 45–50.

CCAFS (Climate Change, Agriculture and Food Security). 2014. "Climate Smart Villages." An Action Research Conducted by CCAFS in West Africa, East Africa and South Asia. http://ccafs.cgiar.org/climate-smart-villages#.VHWw4MJ00y-.

CCC (Climate Change Cell). 2009a. *Climate Change, Gender and Vulnerable Groups in Bangladesh.* DoE, MoEF; Component 4b, CDMP, MoFDM.

CCC (Climate Change Cell). 2009b. *Environment Cost for Climate Change.* DoE, MoEF; Component 4b, CDMP, MoFDM.

CCC (Climate Change Cell). 2007. *Climate Change and Bangladesh.* Department of Environment, Government of the People's Republic of Bangladesh (GoB).

ccGAP (Climate Change and Gender Action Plan). 2013. Ministry of Environment and Forest, Government of Bangladesh (GoB) and IUCN, Global Gender Climate Alliance.

CDMP (Comprehensive Disaster Management Programme II). 2014a. *Development of Four Decade Long Climate Change and Trend: Temperature, Rainfall, Sunshine and Humidity.* Ministry of Disaster Management and Relief, Government of Bangladesh (GoB).

CDMP (Comprehensive Disaster Management Programme II). 2014b. *Trend and Impact Analysis of Internal Displacement Due to the Impacts of Disaster and Climate Change.* Ministry of Disaster Management and Relief, Government of Bangladesh (GoB).

CDMP (Comprehensive Disaster Management Programme II). 2014c. *Policy Brief: Local Level Hazards for Flood, Storm Surge and Salinity.* Ministry of Disaster Management and Relief, Government of Bangladesh (GoB).

CDMP (Comprehensive Disaster Management Programme II). 2013. *Climate Induced Drought: Scenario and Impacts.* Ministry of Disaster Management and Relief. Government of Bangladesh (GoB).

CDMP (Comprehensive Disaster Management Programme II). 2012a. *Report on the Landslide Inventory & Land Use Mapping, DEM Preparation, Precipitation Threshold Value and Establishment of Early Warning Devices.* Ministry of Disaster Management and Relief, Government of Bangladesh (GoB).

CDMP (Comprehensive Disaster Management Programme II). 2012b. *Report on the Landslide Hazard Zonation Mapping at Cox's Bazar and Teknaf in Bangladesh.* Ministry of Disaster Management and Relief, Government of Bangladesh (GoB).

CDMP (Comprehensive Disaster Management Programme II). 2012c. *Final Report on the Rainfall Triggered Landslide Hazard Zonation Mapping at Cox's Bazar and Teknaf Municipalities as Well as Introducing Community-Based Early Warning System for Landslide Hazard Management.* Ministry of Disaster Management and Relief, Government of Bangladesh (GoB).

CDMP II (Comprehensive Disaster Management Programme). 2010. *Project Brief: Ministry of Disaster Management and Relief.* Government of Peoples Republic Bangladesh.

Choudhury, A., S. Neelormi, D. Quadir, S. Mallick, and A. U. Ahmed. 2005. "Socioeconomic and Physical Perspectives of Water Related Vulnerability to Climate Change: Results of Field Study in Bangladesh." *Science and Culture* 71 (7–8): 225.

Chowdhury, A. 2012. "Climate Change Finance and Governance: Bangladesh Perspectives." IGS Working Paper Series No. 02/2012. The Institute of Governance Studies, BRAC University.

Chowdhury, F. 2009. "Theorising Patriarchy: The Bangladesh Context." *Asian Journal of Social Science* 37 (4): 599–622.

Chowdhury, H. 2015. "Bangladesh Evacuates 300,000 People as Cyclone 'Komen' Approaches." bdnews24.com, July 30.

Christensen, A., R. Hilda, M. Breengaard, and H. Oldrup. 2009. "Gendering Climate Change." *Women, Gender and Research* 3 (3): 3–9.

Cyclone Preparedness Program. 2014. "Bangladesh Red Crescent Society." http://www.cpp.gov.bd.

Dankelman, I. 2008. "Introduction: Exploring Gender, Environment and Climate Change." In *Understanding the Linkages, Gender and Climate Change: An Introduction*, edited by I. Dankelman. Earthscan.

Dankelman, I. 2002. "Climate Change: Learning from Gender Analysis and Women's Experiences of Organising for Sustainable Development." *Gender & Development* 10 (2): 21–29.

Dankelman, I., and J. Davidson. 1988. *Women and Environment in the Third World:* Alliance for the Future. Routledge.

Das, P. 2014. "Women's Participation in Community-Level Water Governance in Urban India: The Gap between Motivation and Ability." *World Development* 64: 206–218.

Dastagir, R. 2015. "Modeling Recent Climate Change Induced Extreme Events in Bangladesh: A Review." *Weather and Climate Extreme* 7: 49–60.

Delaporte, I., and M. Maurel. 2016. "Adaptation to Climate Change in Bangladesh." FERDI Working Paper, No. P145, Fondation pour les études et recherches sur le développement international (FERDI).

Denton, F. 2002. "Climate Change Vulnerability, Impacts and Adaptation: Why Does Gender Matter?" *Gender and Development* 10 (2): 10–20.

Disaster Management Bureau, Ministry of Food and Disaster Management, Government of Bangladesh (GoB). 2011. *Bangladesh Disaster Report.* GoB.

Displacement Solutions. 2012. *Climate Displacement in Bangladesh: The Need for Urgent Housing, Land and Property (HLP) Rights Solutions*. Displacement Solutions.

Dobscha, S. 1993. "Women and the Environment: Applying Ecofeminism to Environmentally-Related Consumption." *Advances in Consumer Research* 20 (1): 36–40.

Easterling, W., P. Aggarwal, P. Batima, K. Brander, L. Erda, M. Howden, A. Kirilenko, J. Morton, J.-F. Soussana, S. Schmidhuber, and F. Tubiello. 2007. "Food, Fibre, and Forest Products." In *Climate Change 2007: Impacts, Adaptation and Vulnerability*, edited by M. L. Parry, O. F. Canziani, J. P. Palutikof, P. van der Linden, and C. E. Hanson. Cambridge University Press.

Ekpoh, I. J. 1999. "Estimating the Sensitivity of Crop Yields to Potential Climate Change in the North–Western Nigeria." *Global Journal of Pure and Applied Sciences* 5 (3): 303–308.

Elmhirst, R. 2011. "Introducing New Feminist Political Ecologies." *Geoforum* 42 (2): 129–132.

Enarson, E. 2012. *Women Confronting Natural Disaster: From Vulnerability to Resilience*. Lynne Reinner Publishers.

Enarson, E., and B. H. Morrow. 1998. *The Gendered Terrain of Disaster: Through Women's Eyes*. Praeger.

Epstein, E. 2015. "How One Architect Transformed Education in Flood-Ravaged Bangladesh through 'Floating Schools.' " Mashable Australia. http://mashable.com/2015/07/21/bangladesh-floating-schools/.

Eunice, A., and S. Gry. 2011. "Women: Key to Food Security and Climate Change." *Appropriate Technology* 38 (4): 40–42.

Faeth, P., and E. Weinthal. 2012. "How Access to Clean Water Prevents Conflict." *Solutions* 3 (1). https://dlc.dlib.indiana.edu/dlcrest/api/core/bitstreams/703ebc99-72be-41c6-94f2-461e7b385d18/content.

Gaard, G. 2015. "Ecofeminism and Climate Change." *Women's Studies International Forum* 49: 20–33.

Gaard, G., and L. Gruen. 2005. "Ecofeminism: Toward Global Justice and Planetary Health." In Environmental Philosophy: From Animal Rights to Radical

Ecology. 4th ed. M. Zimmerman, J. B. Callicott, and J. Clark Zimmerman. Prentice Hall.

GCRI (Global Climate Change Risk Index). 2021. "Briefing Paper: Who Suffers Most from Extreme Weather Events? Weather-Related Loss Events in 2019 and 2019–2021." German Watch. https://www.germanwatch.org/en /19777.

Gebrehiwot, T., and A. Veen. 2013. "Farm Level Adaptation to Climate Change: The Case of Farmer's in the Ethiopian Highlands." *Environmental Management* 52 (1): 29–44.

General Economics Division. 2015. *Millennium Development Goals: Bangladesh Report.* Bangladesh Planning Commission, Government of Peoples Republic Bangladesh (GoB).

Ghafur, A. 1999. *Draft Report on Socio-Economic and Environmental Impact of Shrimp Culture in Southwestern Bangladesh:* An Integrated Approach—Part 1. Research and Development Collective (RDC).

Glazebrook, T. 2011. "Women and Climate Change: A Case Study from Northeast Ghana." *Hypatia* 26 (4): 762–782.

Goh, A. H. X. 2012. "A Literature Review of the Gender-Differentiated Impacts of Climate Change on Women's and Men's Assets and Well-Being in Developing Countries." CAPRi Working Paper No. 106. International Food Policy Research Institute. http://doi.org/10.2499/CAPRiWP106

Government of the People's Republic of Bangladesh. 2011. *National Women's Development Policy–2011.* Ministry of Women and Children Affairs.

Government of the People's Republic of Bangladesh. 2009. *Bangladesh Climate Change Strategy Action Plan.* Ministry of Environment and Forest.

Gray, C. L., and V. Mueller. 2012. "Natural Disasters and Population Mobility in Bangladesh." *PNAS* 109 (16): 6000–6005.

Griffin, C. 2004. "The Advantages and Limitations of Qualitative Research." *Psychology and Education* 2: 3–15.

Griffin, S. 1997. "Ecofeminism and Meaning." In *Ecofeminism: Women, Nature and Culture*, edited by Karen Warren. Indiana University Press.

Guhathakurta, M. 2003. "Globalization, Gender and Class Relations." In *Globalization, Environmental Crisis and Social Change in Bangladesh*, edited by M. Rahman. University Press (UPL).

Habiba, U., R. Hassan, and R. Shaw. 2013. "Livelihood Adaptation in the Drought Prone Areas of Bangladesh." In *Climate Change Adaptation Actions in Bangladesh*, edited by R. Shaw, F. Mallick, and A. Islam. Springer.

Habiba, U., R. Shaw, and Y. Takeuchi. 2012. "Farmer's Preconception and Adaptation Practices to Cope with Drought: Perspectives from Northwestern Bangladesh." *International Journal of Disaster Risk Reduction* 1: 72–84.

Habibullah, M., U. Ahmed, and Z. Karim, 1999. "Assessment of Food Grain Production Loss Due to Climate Induced Enhanced Soil Salinity." In *Vulnerability and Adaptation to Climate Change for Bangladesh*, edited by S. Huq, et al. Springer.

Haque, M. F., M. A. R. Sarker, M. S. Rahman, and M. Rakibuddin. 2020. "Discrimination of Women at RMG Sector in Bangladesh." *Journal of Social and Political Sciences* 3 (1) 112–118.

Haque, U., M. Hashizume, N. Kolivras, J. Overgaard, B. Das, and T. Yamamoto. 2012. "Reduced Death Rates from Cyclones in Bangladesh: What More Needs to Be Done?" *Bulletin of the World Health Organization* 90 (2): 77–156.

Hasan, M. 2015. "Bangladesh's Climate Change Migrants." *IRIN*, November 13.

Hassan, M., and M. Shahnewaz. 2014. "Measuring Tourist Service Satisfaction at Destination: A Case Study of Cox's Bazar Sea Beach." *American Journal of Tourism Management* 3 (1): 32–43.

Hawkins, R., and D. Ojeda. 2011. "Gender and Environment: Critical Tradition and New Challenges." *Environment and Planning D: Society and Space* 29 (2): 237–253.

HIES (Household Income Expenditure Survey). 2022. *Bangladesh Bureau of Statistics (BBS) Statistics and Informatics Division (SID)*. Ministry of Planning. Government of Bangladesh. https://bbs.portal.gov.bd.

Hijioka, Y., E. Lin, J. J. Pereira, R. T. Corlett, X. Cui, G. E. Insarov, R. D. Lasco, E. Lindgren, and A. Surjan. 2014. "Asia." In *Climate Change 2014: Impacts, Adaptation, and Vulnerability. Part B: Regional Aspects. Contribution of Working Group II to the Fifth Assessment Report of the Intergovernmental Panel on Climate Change*, edited by Christopher B. Field and Vicente R. Barros. Cambridge University Press.

Hossain, N., and N. Kabeer. 2004. "Achieving Universal Primary Education and Eliminating Gender Disparity." *Economic and Political Weekly* September 4: 4093–4098.

Hovorka, A. 2006. "The No. 1 Ladies' Poultry Farm: A Feminist Political Ecology of Urban Agriculture in Botswana." *Gender, Place and Culture* 13 (3): 207–255.

Hsieh, H.-F. and E. Shannon. 2005. "Three Approaches to Qualitative Content Analysis." *Qualitative Health Research* 15 (9): 1277–1288.

IISS (International Institute for Strategic Studies). 2000. "Weather and Security: Climate and South Asia." *Strategic Comments* 6 (1): 1–2.

IPCC (Intergovernmental Panel on Climate Change). 2023. "Summary for Policymakers." In *Climate Change 2023: Synthesis Report*. Contribution of Working Groups I, II and III to the Sixth Assessment Report of the Intergovernmental Panel on Climate Change [Core Writing Team, H. Lee and J. Romero (eds.)]. IPCC.

IPCC (Intergovernmental Panel on Climate Change). 2014. *Climate Change 2014: Synthesis Report*. IPCC.

IPCC (Intergovernmental Panel on Climate Change). 2007. *Climate Change: Impact, Adaptation and Vulnerability*. Contribution of Working Group II to the Fourth Assessment Report. IPCC.

Irfanullah, M. H., K. Azad, M. Kamruzzam, and A. Wahed. 2011. "Floating Garden in Bangladesh: A Means to Rebuild Lives after Devastating Flood." *Indian Journal of Traditional Knowledge* 10 (1): 31–38.

Islam, A. 2015. "Heterogeneous Effects of Microcredit: Evidence from Large-Scale Programs in Bangladesh." *Journal of Asian Economics* 37: 48–58.

Islam, A., and A. Sumon. 2013. "Integration of Climate Change Adaptation, Disaster Risk Reduction and Social Protection in Bangladesh: Contemporary Views and Experiences." In *Climate Change Adaptation Actions in Bangladesh*, edited by R. Shaw, F. Mallick, and A. Islam. Springer.

Islam, F., H. Hove, and J. Parry. 2011. *Review of Current and Planned Adaptation Action: South Asia (Afghanistan, Bangladesh, Bhutan, India, Maldives, Nepal, Pakistan and Sri Lanka)*. International Institute for Sustainable Development.

Islam, T., and E. Peterson. 2009. "Climatology of Landfalling Tropical Cyclones in Bangladesh 1877–2003." *Natural Hazards* 48 (1): 115–135.

Jackson, C. 1993. "Women/Nature or Gender/History? A Critique of Ecofeminist Development." *Journal of Peasant Studies* 20 (3): 384–419.

Jahan, M. 2008. "The Impact of Environmental Degradation on Women in Bangladesh: An Overview." *Asian Affairs Journal* 30 (2): 5–15.

Kabeer, N. 1988. "Subordination and Struggle: Women in Bangladesh." *New Left Review* 168 (1): 95–121.

Kabeer, N., and S. Mahmud. 2004. "Globalization, Gender and Poverty: Bangladeshi Women Workers in Export and Local Markets." *Journal of International Development* 16 (1): 93–109.

Kabir, E. 2012. "Shrimp Culture and Feminist Environmentalism: A Case Study from Bangladesh." *Bangladesh Journal of Public Administration* XXI (1): 63–76.

Karim, F., and N. Mimura. 2008. "Impacts of Climate Change and Sea-Level Rise on Cyclonic Storm Surge Floods in Bangladesh." *Global Environmental Change* 18 (3): 490–500.

Karim, N. 1995. "Disasters in Bangladesh." *Natural Hazards* 11 (3): 247–258.

Karim, Z. 2013. "Women's Property Rights in Bangladesh: What Is Practically Happening in South Asian Rural Communities." *Social Sciences* 8 (2): 160–165.

Karim, Z., A. M. Ibrahim, A. Iqbal, and M. Ahmed. 1990. "Drought in Bangladesh Agriculture and Irrigation Schedules for Major Crops." Bangladesh Agricultural Research Council (BARC), Soils Public. No. 34, 11.

Kartiki, K. 2011. "Climate Change and Migration: A Case Study from Rural Bangladesh." *Gender and Development* 19 (1): 23–38.

Kevany, K., and D. Huisingh. 2013. "A Review of Progress in Empowerment of Women in Rural Water Management Decision-Making Processes." *Journal of Cleaner Production* 60: 53–64.

Khan, M. H., and A. Kraemer. 2008. "Socio-Economic Factors Explain Differences in Public Health-Related Variables Among Women in Bangladesh: A Cross-Sectional Study." *BMC Public Health* 8 (1): 254.

Khan, R., and A. Rahman. 2007. "Partnership Approach to Disaster Management in Bangladesh: A Critical Policy Assessment." *Natural Hazards* 41 (2): 359–378.

Khandker, S. R. 2012. "Seasonality of Income and Poverty in Bangladesh." *Journal of Development Economics* 97 (2): 244–256.

King, G., R. O. Keohane, and S. Verba. 1994. *Designing Social Inquiry: Scientific Inference in Qualitative Research*. Princeton University Press.

King, Y. 1989. "The Ecology of Feminism and the Feminism of Ecology." In *Healing the Wounds: The Promise of Ecofeminism*, edited by J. Plant. New Society Publishers.

Kipot, E., S. Franzel, and A. Degrande. 2014. "Gender Agroforestry and Food Security in Africa." *Environmental Sustainability* 6: 104–109.

Kjekstad, O., and L. Highland. 2009. "Economic and Social Impacts of Landslides." In *Landslides—Disaster Risk Reduction*, edited by K. Sassa and P. Canuti. Springer.

Konate, M., and Y. Sokona. 2003. "Mainstreaming Adaptation to Climate Change in Least Developed Countries." Working Paper 3, Mali Country Case Study, IIED (International Institute for Environment and Development).

Kronsell, A. 2013. "Gender and Transition in Climate Governance." *Environmental Innovation and Societal Transitions* 7: 1–15.

Kuruppu, N. 2009. "Adapting Water Resources to Climate Change in Kiribati: The Importance of Cultural Values and Meanings." *Environmental Science and Policy* 12 (7): 799–809.

Lacey, A., and L. Donna. 2007 *Qualitative Data Analysis*. The NIHR Research Design Service for the East Midlands/Yorkshire & Humber.

Leach, M. 2007. "Earth Mother Myths and Other Ecofeminist Fables: How a Strategic Notion Rose and Fell." *Development and Change* 38 (1): 67–85.

Leonard, S., M. Parsons, K. Olawsky, and F. Kofod. 2013. "The Role of Culture and Traditional Knowledge in Climate Change Adaptation: Insights from East Kimberley, Australia." *Global Environmental Change* 23 (3): 623–632.

(LGD), Ministry of Local Government and Rural Development & Cooperatives, Government of Bangladesh (GoB).

Liberman, S. 2005. "Nested Analysis as a Mixed-Method Strategy for Comparative Research." *American Political Science Review* 99 (3): 435–452.

Loro, L. 2013. *Women's Empowerment as a Result of Microcredit Loans in Bangladesh?* Bangladesh Development Research Centre (BDRC).

Luxbacher, K. 2011. "Bangladesh Comprehensive Disaster Management Programme. CDKN Inside Stories on Climate Compatible Development, Climate and Development Knowledge Network."

MacGregor, S. 2009. "Natural Allies, Perennial Foes? On the Trajectories of Feminist and Green Political Thought." *Contemporary Political Theory* 8 (3): 329–339.

MacGregor, S. 2005. "The Public, the Private, the Planet and the Province: Women's Quality of Life Activism in Urban Southern Ontario." In *This Elusive Land: Women and the Canadian Environment*, edited by M. Hessing, R. Raglan, and C. Sandilands. University of British Columbia Press.

Mahmood, N., P. Dhakal, and R. Keast. 2014. "The State of Multi-Purpose Cyclone Shelters in Bangladesh." *Facilities* 32 (9–10): 522–532.

Mahmood, B., and H. Khan. 2008. "Landslide Vulnerability of Bangladesh Hills and Sustainable Management Options: A Case Study of 2007 Landslide in Chittagong City." International Seminar on Management and Mitigation of Water Induced Disaster, Kathmandu, Nepal, April 28, 2008.

Mahtab, F., ed. *Vulnerability and Adaptation to Climate Change for Bangladesh.* Kluwer Academic Publishers.

Mallick, B., and J. Vogt. 2014. "Population Displacement after Cyclone and Its Consequences: Empirical Evidence from Coastal Bangladesh." *Natural Hazards* 73 (2): 191–212.

Mallory, C. 2010. "What Is Ecofeminist Political Philosophy? Gender, Nature, and the Political." Environmental Ethics 32 (3): 306–322.

Martin, B. 2006. *Mimetic Moments: Adorno and Ecofeminism*. Pennsylvania State University Press.

McCright, A. M. 2010. "The Effects of Gender on Climate Change Knowledge and Concern in the American Public." *Population and Environment* 32 (1): 66–87.

MDMP (Municipality Disaster Management Plan). 2014. *Cox's Bazar Disaster Management Committee*. CDPM-II and MoDMR.

Mellor, A. K. 1997. "Romanticism, Gender, and the Anxieties of Empire: An Introduction." *European Romantic Review* 8 (2): 148–154.

Merchant, C. 1992. *Radical Ecology: The Search for a Liveable World*. Routledge.

Mies, M., and V. Shiva. 2014. *Ecofeminism: Critique, Influence and Change*. 2nd ed. Zed Books.

Milne, W. 2005. "Changing Climate, Uncertain Future: Considering Rural Women in Climate Changes Policies and Strategies." *Canadian Woman Studies* 24 (4): 49–54.

Mirza, Q. M. 2002. "Global Warming and Changes in the Probability of Occurrence of Floods in Bangladesh and Implications." *Global Environmental Change* 12 (2): 127–138.

Mirza, Q., A. Warrick, and J. Ericksen. 2003. "The Implications of Climate Change on Floods of the Ganges, Bramhaputra and Meghna Rivers in Bangladesh." *Climate Change* 57 (3): 287–318.

MoDMR (Ministry of Disaster Management and Relief). 2015. *Management Lessons Learned: Reviewing Disasters Over 10 Years: 2005–2015*. Bangladesh's Disaster, Ministry of Disaster Management and Relief. Government of Bangladesh (GoB).

MoDMR (Ministry of Disaster Management and Relief) and UNDP. 2004. *Documents on Comprehensive Disaster Management Project*. Government of Bangladesh (GoB).

MoEFCC (Ministry of Environment, Forest and Climate Change). n.d. Climate Change and Gender in Bangladesh, Information Brief. MoEFCC.

MoFDM (Ministry of Food and Disaster Management). 2010. *Bangladesh National Plan for Disaster Management (2010–2015)*. Government of Bangladesh (GoB).

Mohsin, A. 2010. "Coming Out of the Private: Women Forging Voices in Bangladesh." In *Mapping Women's Empowerment: Experiences from Bangladesh, India and Pakistan*, edited by A. Firdous and M. Sultan. UPL & BDI.

Moni, J. 2016. "Krishite Barchhe Narir Bhumika" [Women's Contribution in Agriculture Is Increasing]. *Daily Prothom Alo*, January 14.

Morol, S. 2015. "Ma o Shishu Sasther Jhuki Barachhe Lona Pani" [Salinity Water Is Increasing the Health Hazards of Mother and Children: A Study on Pregnant Women]. *Daily Prothom Alo*, November 17.

Nandy, P., R. Ahammad, M. Alam, and A. Islam. 2013. "Coastal Ecosystem Based Adaptation: Bangladesh Experience." In *Climate Change Adaptation Actions in Bangladesh*, edited by R. Shaw, F. Mallick, and A. Islam. Springer.

NAP (National Adaption Plan of Bangladesh). 2022. *Ministry of Environment, Forest and Climate Change*. Government of the People's Republic of Bangladesh.

NAPA (National Adaptation Programme of Action). 2005. Ministry of Environment and Forest. Government of the People's Republic of Bangladesh (GoB).

Nasreen, M. 2012. *Women and Girls: Vulnerable or Resilient?* Institute of Disaster Management and Vulnerability Studies, University of Dhaka.

Nasreen, M. 2010. "Rethinking Disaster Management: Violence against Women During Floods in Bangladesh." In *Women's Encounter with Disasters*, edited by S. Dasgupta, et al. FrontPage Publications.

Nasreen, M. 2008a. *Impact of Climate Change on Agriculture and Food Security*. ActionAid International and ActionAid Bangladesh.

Nasreen, M. 2008b. *Violence against Women During Disaster and Post-Disaster Situations in Bangladesh*. ActionAid International and ActionAid Bangladesh.

Nasreen, M., M. Hossain, and K. Azad. 2013. "Climate Change and Livelihood in Bangladesh: Experiences of People Living in Coastal Regions." Paper presented at the International Conference Building Resilience: Individual, Institutional and Societal Coping Strategies to Address the Challenges Associated with Disaster Risk, Herritance Ahungalla, Sri Lanka, September 17–19, 2013.

Nasrin, F. 2012. "Women, Environment and Environmental Advocacy: Challenges for Bangladesh." *Asian Journal of Social Sciences & Humanities* 1 (3): 149–172.

National Plan for Disaster Management (2010–2015). Disaster Management Bureau, Disaster Management & Relief Division. GOB.

Neelormi, S. 2010. "Addressing Gender Issues in Adaptation." In *Reducing Vulnerability to Climate Change: The Pioneering Example of Community-Based Adaptation*, edited by A. U. Ahmed. Centre for Global Change and CARE Bangladesh.

Neelormi, S., A. Adri, and U. A. Ahmed. 2009. "Gender Dimensions of Differential Health Effects of Climate Change Induced Water-Logging: A Case Study from Coastal Bangladesh." *IOP Conference Series Earth and Environmental Science* 6: 1420026.

Neelormi, S., and U. A. Ahmed. 2012. *Loss and Damage in a Warmer World: Whither Gender Matters, Gender Perspective on the Loss and Damage Debate*. Climate and Development Knowledge Network (CDKN).

Nightingale, A. 2006. "The Nature of Gender: Work, Gender, and Environment." *Environment and Planning: Society and Space* 24 (2): 165–185.

NIOPORT (National Institute of Population Research and Training). 2013. *Bangladesh Demographic and Population Health Survey*. NIOPORT.

Nyong, A., F. Adesina, and E. B. Osman. 2007. "The Value of Indigenous Knowledge in Climate Change Mitigation and Adaptation Strategies in the African Sahel." *Mitigation and Adaptation Strategies for Global Change* 12 (5): 787–797.

O'Brien, G., P. O'Keefe, J. Rose, and B. Wisner. 2006. "Climate Change and Disaster Management." *Disasters* 30 (1): 64–80.

O'Brien, M., and T. D. Holland. 1992. "The Role of Adaptation in Archaeological Explanation." *American Antiquity* 57: 36–69.

Panda, A. M. 2007. "Mainstreaming Gender in Water Management: A Critical View." *Gender, Technology & Development* 11 (3), 321–338.

Paul, B. K. 1998. "Coping Mechanisms Practised by Drought Victims (1994/5) in North Bengal, Bangladesh." *Applied Geography* 18 (4): 355–373.

Paul, B. K. 1995. "Farmers and Public Responses to the 1994–95 Drought in Bangladesh: A Case Study". Paper 79, Natural Hazards Research and Applications Information Center, University of Colorado.

Perucca, C. 2011. *Social Water Management among Indigenous Munda in Sundarban*. IPMCC.

Pouliotte, J., B. Smit, and L. Westerhoff. 2009. "Adaptation and Development: Livelihoods and Climate Change in Subarnabad, Bangladesh." *Climate and Development* 1 (1): 31–46.

Qin, H. 2010. "Rural-to-Urban Labour Migration, Household Livelihoods, and the Rural Environment in Chongqing Municipality, Southwest China." *Human Ecology* 38 (5): 675–690.

Rahman, A., and J. McAllister. 2011. *Microcredit and Women's Empowerment: A Case Study of Bangladesh*. Routledge.

Rahman, I. R., and R. Islam. 2013. "Female Labour Force Participation in Bangladesh: Trends, Drivers and Barriers." ILO Asia-Pacific Working Paper Series. DWT for South Asia and Country Office for India.

Rahman, M. 2012. "Gender-Positive Changes in Benefit-Sharing in Social Forestry Projects in Bangladesh, Bhutan+10." Gender and Sustainable Mountain Development in a Changing World International Conference, Timphu, Bhutan, October 15–19, 2012.

Rahman, M. M., and A. Q. M. Mahbub. 2012. "Groundwater Depletion with Expansion of Irrigation in Barind Tract: A Case Study of Tanore Upazila." *Journal of Water Resource and Protection* 4 (8): 567–575.

Rahman, R., and M. Asaduzzman. 2010. "Ecology of Sundarban." *Bangladesh. Journal of Science Foundation* 8 (1–2): 35–47.

Rahman, S. 2012. "Upazila Parishad in Bangladesh: Roles and Functions of Elected Representatives and Bureaucrats." *Commonwealth Journal of Local Governance*, December 11: 100–117.

Rahman, Z., A. Choudury, and S. Ali. 2012. *Social Safety Nets in Bangladesh: Review of Issues and Analytical Inventory*, vol. 1. Power and Participation Research Centre (PPRC) and United Nations Development Programme (UNDP).

Raihan, H. M., N. Islam, A. Rouf, A. Begum, M. Rahman, S. Murad, and S. Das. 2014. "Health Care Situation of Migrant Slum Women: Evidence from Sylhet City of Bangladesh." *Bangladesh e-Journal of Sociology* 11 (1): 119–134.

Raj, P., and P. Gain. 1998. "Citizen's Responses to Environmental Issues." In *Bangladesh Environment: Facing the 21st Century*, edited P. Gain. SEHD.

Rangan, H. 2000. *Of Myths and Movements: Rewriting Chipko into Himalayan History.* Verso.

Rashid, H. n.d. "Cyclone Preparedness Programme (CPP) Bangladesh Red Crescent Society." Concept Paper. http://www.iawe.org/WRDRR_Bangladesh/Preprints/S4CPP.pdf.

Rashid, M. 2009. *Climate Change and Vulnerability in Bangladesh: Strategic Position of DSK/DCA in the Field of Climate Change Adaptation Initiatives in Bangladesh.* Dustha Shansta Kendra (DSK) and Dan Church Aid (DCA).

Rashid, S. F. and S. Michaud. 2000. "Female Adolescents and Their Sexuality: Notions of Honour, Shame, Purity and Pollution During the Floods." *Disasters* 24 (1): 54–70.

Resurrección, B. P. 2013. "Persistent Women and Environment Linkages in Climate Change and Sustainable Development Agendas." *Women's Studies International Forum* 40: 33–43.

Resurrección, B. P., and R. Elmhirst, eds. 2008. *Gender and Natural Resource Management: Livelihoods, Mobility and Interventions.* Earthscan.

Rocheleau, D. E. 1995. "Gender and Biodiversity: A Feminist Political Ecology Perspective." *IDS Bulletin* 26 (1): 9–16.

Rocheleau, D. E., and D. Edmunds. 1997. "Women, Men and Trees: Gender, Power and Property in Forest and Agrarian Landscapes." *World Development* 25 (8): 1351–1371.

Rocheleau, D. E., B. Thomas-Slayter, and E. Wangari. 1996. "Feminist Politics and Environmental Justice." In *Feminist Political Ecology: Global Issues and Local Experiences*, edited by D. Rocheleau, B. Thomas-Stayler, and E. Wangari. Routledge.

Rodda, A. 1991. *Women and the Environment.* Zed Books.

Rodima-Taylor, D., M. F. Olwig, and N. Chhetri. 2012. "Adaptation as Innovation, Innovation as Adaptation: An Institutional Approach to Climate Change." *Applied Geography* 33: 107–111.

Roos, V., S. Chigeza, and D. Van Niekerk. 2010. "Coping with Drought: Indigenous Knowledge Application in Rural South Africa." *Indilinga–African Journal of Indigenous Knowledge Systems* 9 (1): 1–11.

Rose, S., N. Spinks, and I. Canhoto. 2014. *Management Research: Applying the Principles.* Routledge.

Rowley, J. 2002. "Using Case Studies in Research." *Management Research News* 25 (1): 16–27.

Ruane, C., C. Major, H. Winston, M. Alam, G. Hussain, S. Khan, A. Hassan, B. Md. Tamim Al Hossain, R. Goldberg, R. M. Horton, and C. Rosenzweig. 2013. "Multi-Factor Impact Analysis of Agricultural Production in Bangladesh with Climate Change." *Global Environmental Change* 23 (1): 338–350.

Sachs, C. 1996. *Gendered Fields: Rural Women, Agriculture, and Environment.* Westview Press.

Salehi, S., P. Z. Nejad, H. Mahmoudi, and A. Knierim. 2015. "Gender, Responsible Citizenship and Global Climate Change." *Women's Studies International Forum* 50: 30–36.

Scalise, E. 2009. *Women's Inheritance Rights to Land and Property in South Asia: A Study of Afghanistan, Bangladesh, India, Nepal, Pakistan, and Sri Lanka.* A Report by the Rural Development Institute (RDI) for the World Justice Project.

Seager, J. 1993. Earth Follies: *Coming to Feminist Terms with the Global Environmental Crisis.* Routledge.

Selam, O. 2010. *Ecofeminism or Death.* Doctoral diss., Binghamton University, State University of New York.

Selvaraju, R., A. R. Subbiah, S. Baas, and I. Juergens. 2006. "Livelihood Adaptation to Climate Variability and Change in Drought-Prone Areas of Bangladesh: Developing Institutions and Options." DP9/1-BGD/01/004/01/99. Asian Disaster Preparedness Center and Food and Agriculture Organization.

Shabib, D., and S. Khan. 2014. "Gender-Sensitive Adaptation Policy-Making in Bangladesh: Status and Ways Forward for Improved Mainstreaming." *Climate and Development* 6 (4): 329–335.

Shahid, S. 2008. "Spatial and Temporal Characteristics of Droughts in the Western Part of Bangladesh." *Hydrological Processes* 22 (13): 2235–2247.

Shahid, S., and H. Behrawan. 2008. "Drought Risk Assessment in the Western Part of Bangladesh." *Natural Hazards* 46 (3): 391–413.

Shamsuddoha, S., H. M. Khan, S. Raihan, and T. Hossain. 2012. *Displacement and Migration from Climate Hot-Spots in Bangladesh: Causes and Consequences.* Action Aid Bangladesh.

Shields, D., B. Flora, B. Thomas-Slayter, and G. Buenavista. 1996. "Feminist Political Ecology: Cross Cutting Themes, Theoretical Insights, Policy Implication." In *Feminist Political Ecology: Global Issues and Local Experiences,* edited by D. Rocheleau, B. Thomas-Slayter, and E. Wangari. Routledge.

Shiva, V. 1993. "The Chipko Women's Concept of Freedom." In *Ecofeminism,* edited by M. Mies and V. Shiva. Zed Books.

Shiva, V. 1989. *Staying Alive: Women, Ecology and Survival in India.* Zed Books.

SHOUHARDO II. 2011. Winners' Wisdom: *Indigenous Coping Practices in Disaster Management in Bangladesh.* CARE Bangladesh.

Silvey, R., and R. Elmhirst. 2003. "Engendering Social Capital: Women Workers and Rural-Urban Networks in Indonesia's Crisis." World Development 31 (5): 865–879.

SoD (Standing Orders on Disaster). 2010. *Ministry of Food and Disaster Management.* Government of Bangladesh (GoB).

SOUHARDO II. 2011. *Winners' Wisdom: Indigenous Coping Practices in Disaster Management in Bangladesh.* CARE Bangladesh.

Sovacool, K., L. D'Agostino, A. Rawlani, and H. Meenawat. 2012. "Improving Climate Change Adaptation in Least Developed Asia." *Environmental Science and Policy* 21: 112–125.

Sudarshan, M., and M. Bisht. 2010. " 'Voice' as a Pathway to Women's Empowerment: Reflections on the Indian Experience." In *Mapping Women's Empowerment: Experiences from Bangladesh, India and Pakistan*, edited F. Azim and M. Sultan. UPL & BDI.

Sultan, M. 2010. "Work for Pay and Women's Empowerment: Bangladesh." In *Mapping Women's Empowerment: Experiences from Bangladesh, India and Pakistan*, edited by F. Azim and M. Sultan. UPL & BDI.

Sundberg, J. 2015. "Ethics, Entanglement and Political Ecology." In *The Routledge Handbook of Political Ecology*, edited by T. Perreault, G. Bridge, and J. McCarthy. Routledge.

Tanjeela, M. 2008. *Women's Voice in Local Government Bodies of Bangladesh.* Lambert Academic Publishing.

Tanjeela, M., and M. Billah. 2022. "Climate Migration and Challenges of Urban Poor in Bangladesh." *International Journal of Climate Change: Impacts and Responses* 15 (1): 2022. https://doi.org/10.18848/1835-7156/CGP/v15i01/15-31.

Tariqul, H., S. Farjana, and M. Mujtaba. 2015. "Climate Change, Natural Disaster and Vulnerability to Occupational Changes in Coastal Region of Bangladesh." *Journal of Geography & Natural Disasters* 5: 134.

Terry, G., 2009. "No Climate Justice without Gender Justice: An Overview of the Issues." *Gender and Development* 17 (1): 5–18.

Thomalla, F., T. Cannon, S. Huq, A. J. T. Klein, and C. Schaerer. 2005. "Mainstreaming Adaptation to Climate Change in Coastal Bangladesh by Building Civil Society Alliances." *International Institute for Environment and Development* 176 (67): 668–684.

Thomas-Slayter, B., E. Wangari, and D. Rocheleau. 1996. "Feminist Political Ecology: Cross Cutting Themes, Theoretical Insights, Policy Implication." In *Feminist Political Ecology: Global Issues and Local Experiences*, edited by D. Rocheleau, B. Thomas-Slayter, and E. Wangari. Routledge.

Tompkins, L., and N. Adger. 2004. "Does Adaptive Management of Natural Resources Enhance Resilience to Climate Change?" *Ecology and Society* 9 (2): 10.

UDMP (Upazila Disaster Management Plan). 2014a. *Mongla Upazila Disaster Management Committee.* CDPM-II & MoDMR.

UDMP (Upazila Disaster Management Plan). 2014b. *Dacope Upazila Disaster Management Committee.* CDPM-II & MoDMR.

UDMP (Upazila Disaster Management Plan) 2014c. *Shapahar Upazila Disaster Management Committee.* CDPM-II & MoDMR.

UDMP (Upazila Disaster Management Plan). 2014d. *Gopalgonj Upazila Disaster Management Committee.* CDPM-II & MoDMR.

UNDP (United Nations Development Program). 2014. *The 2014 Human Development Report—Sustaining Human Progress: Reducing Vulnerabilities and Building Resilience; Gender Equality Index-Table 4*. UNDP.

UNDP (United Nations Development Programme). 2010. *Environment and Energy: Community Based Adaptation to Climate Change through Coastal Afforestation in Bangladesh (CBACC-CF Project): Bangladesh Case Study*. UNDP.

UNDP (United Nations Development Programme). 2007. *Human Development Report (2007/2008)*. Fighting Climate Change: Human Solidarity in a Divided World.

UNEP (United Nations Environmental Programme). 2015. "Champions of the Earth." https://www.unep.org/news-and-stories/story/bangladesh-prime-minister-wins-top-united-nations-environmental-prize-policy.

UNFPA (United Nations Population Fund). 2002. *Water a Critical Resource*. UNFPA.

UNICEF (The United Nations Children's Fund). 2010. *Situation Assessment and Analysis of Children and Women in Bangladesh*. UNICEF.

UNICEF (The United Nations Children's Fund). 2008. *Women and Girls in Bangladesh*. UNICEF.

UNISDR (United Nations International Strategy for Disaster Reduction). 2008. *Indigenous Knowledge for Disaster Risk Reduction—Good Practices and Lessons Learned from Experiences in the Asia-Pacific Region*. UNISDR. http://www.unisdr.org/files/3646_IndigenousKnowledgeDRR.pdf.

Vyasulu, P. 2001. "Managing the Environment—A Gender Perspective." In *Environmental Management: An Indian Perspective*, edited by N. Chary and V. Vyasulu. Macmillan.

Wangari, E., B. Thomas-Slayter, and D. Rocheleau. 1996. "Gendered Visions for Survival: Semi-Arid Regions in Kenya." In *Feminist Political Ecology: Global Issues and Local Experiences*, edited by D. Rocheleau, et al. Routledge.

WARPO (Water Resources Planning Organizations). 2005. *Impact Assessment of Climate Changes on the Coastal Zones of Bangladesh*. Ministry of Water Resources, Government of Peoples Republic Bangladesh (GoB).

WB (World Bank). 2015. "Emergency 2007 Cyclone Recovery and Restoration Project (P111272) SOUTH ASIA Bangladesh." Agriculture and Rural

Development Global Practice IBRD/IDA, Emergency Recovery Loan FY 2009 Seq No: 13. Archived May 21, 2015. ISR19078.

WB (World Bank). 2012. *4 Turn Down the Heat: Why a 4°C Warmer World Must Be Avoided.* A Report for the World Bank by the Potsdam Institute. http://climateanalytics.org/files/turn_down_the_heat_11-16-12.pdf.

WB (World Bank). 2010. *Economics of Adaptation to Climate Change: Bangladesh.* Country Case Studies. World Bank.

WEDO (Women's Environment and Development Organization). 2008. *Gender, Climate Change and Human Security, Commissioned by the Greek Chairmanship (2007–2008) of the Human Security Network.* The Report Includes Three Country Specific Case Studies Prepared by WEDO Partners; the Other Country Assessments Are of Senegal and Ghana. Case Study: Gender Human Security and Climate Change in Bangladesh.

WEF (World Economic Form). 2023. *The Global Gender Gap Report.* WEF.

World Bank Group. 2010. *Economics of Adaptation to Climate Change.* http://www.worldbank.org/en/news/feature/2011/06/06/economics-adaptation-climate-change.

Yin, R. K. 2014. *Case Study Research: Design and Methods Sage Publications.* 5th ed. Applied Social Research Methods Series 5. SAGE.

Yin, R. K. 2009. *Case Study Research: Design and Methods Sage Publications.* 4th ed. Applied Social Research Methods Series 5. SAGE.

Yin, R. K. 2003. *Case Study Research: Design and Methods Sage Publications.* 3rd ed. Applied Social Research Methods Series 5. SAGE.

Yin, R. K. 1994. *Case Study Research: Design and Methods.* SAGE.

www.ingramcontent.com/pod-product-compliance
Lightning Source LLC
Chambersburg PA
CBHW041935260326
41914CB00010B/1309